gem

Collins
Spanish
phrasebook

Consultant
Lydia Batanaz

First published 1993
This edition published 2010
Copyright © HarperCollins Publishers
Reprint 10 9 8 7 6 5
Typeset by Davidson Publishing Solutions, Glasgow
Printed in China

www.collinslanguage.com

ISBN 978-0-00-735857-1

Using your phrasebook

Your *Collins Gem Phrasebook* is designed to help you locate the exact phrase you need, when you need it, whether on holiday or for business. If you want to adapt the phrases, you can easily see where to substitute your own words using the dictionary section, and the clear, full-colour layout gives you direct access to the different topics.

The Gem Phrasebook includes:

- Over 70 topics arranged thematically. Each phrase is accompanied by a simple pronunciation guide which eliminates any problems pronouncing foreign words.

- A Top ten tips section to safeguard against any cultural faux pas, giving essential dos and don'ts for situations involving local customs or etiquette.

- Practical hints to make your stay trouble free, showing you where to go and what to do when dealing with everyday matters such as travel or hotels and offering valuable tourist information.

- Face to face sections so that you understand what it is being said to you. These example mini-dialogues give you a good idea of what to expect from a real conversation.

- Common announcements and messages you may hear, ensuring that you never miss the important information you need to know when out and about.

- A clearly laid-out 3000-word dictionary means you will never be stuck for words.

- A basic grammar section which will enable you to build on your phrases.

- A list of public holidays to avoid being caught out by unexpected opening and closing hours, and to make sure you don't miss the celebrations!

It's worth spending time before you embark on your travels just looking through the topics to see what is covered and becoming familiar with what might be said to you.

Whatever the situation, your *Gem Phrasebook* is sure to help!

Contents

Pronouncing Spanish

Spelling and pronouncing Spanish are easy once you know the few basic rules. This book has been designed so that as you read the pronunciation of the phrases you can follow the Spanish. This will help you to recognize the different sounds and give you a feeling for the rhythm of the language. The syllable to be stressed is marked in **bold** in the pronunciation. Here are a few rules you should know:

Spanish	sounds like	example	pronunciation
ca	**ka**	cama	**ka**-ma
co	**ko**	con	kon
cu	**ku**	cubo	**koo**bo
ce	**the**	cena	**the**-na
ci	**thee**	cine	**thee**ne
ga	**ga**	gato	**ga**-to
go	**go**	algo	**al**go
gu	**goo**	algún	al**goon**
ge	**khe**	gente	**khen**te
gi	**khee**	giro	**khee**ro
j	**kh**	jueves	**khwe**-bes
ll	**ly**	llamo	**lya**-mo
ñ	**ny**	señor	se-**nyor**
ua	**wa**	cual	kwal

7

Spanish	sounds like	example	pronunciation
ue	**we**	vuelva	**bwel**ba
v	**b**	vuelva	**bwel**ba
z	**th**	Zaragoza	tha-ra-**go**-tha

h is silent: **hora o**-ra, **hola o**-la.
r is rolled and **rr** even more so.

In Spanish, vowels (**a**, **e**, **i**, **o**, **u**) have only one sound. When you find two together, pronounce both of them in quick succession, as in **aceite** a-**they**-te.

Top ten tips

. . . .

1   Greet people with a '**Buenos días**' or
    '**Buenas tardes**' on entering a lift, as it's rude
    not to acknowledge them.

2   Spain is not a queuing country: people do not
    queue in bus stops. In places such as shops,
    banks, markets etc, people ask '**¿quién es el
    último?**' which means 'who is the last one?'

3   When addressing elders or people you have
    been just introduced to, use the formal '**Usted**'
    mode of address.

4   It is normal for people to stand or sit very close
    to each other when talking, which may be
    closer than you're used to. Pulling away from
    your counterpart may be regarded as unfriendly.

5   Taking up spare seats at a table that's already
    occupied is not common.

6   The Spanish do not make a habit of saying
    'please' and 'thank you' very much – it is
    implied in the tone of voice. It is a cultural
    thing, so don't think they are being rude!

7   When you enter a restaurant or a home
    where people are eating, it's polite to say
    'que aproveche', meaning 'enjoy your meal'.

8   If you receive a gift, you should open it
    straightaway and in front of the giver.

9   Expect to be interrupted when speaking!

10 Cover your shoulders and legs when visiting
    religious buildings.

Talking to people

Hello/goodbye, yes/no

The word for Mr is **Señor** (se-**nyor**) and for Mrs/Ms
Señora (se-**nyo**-ra).

Yes	**Sí**
	see
No	**No**
	no
OK!	**¡Vale!**
	¡**ba**-le!
Thank you	**Gracias**
	gra-thyas
Thanks very much	**Muchas gracias**
	moochas **gra**-thyas
Hello	**Hola**
	o-la
Goodbye	**Adiós**
	a-**dyos**
Good night	**Buenas noches**
	bwe-nas **no**-ches

11

Good morning	**Buenos días**
	bwe-nos **dee**-as
Good evening	**Buenas tardes**
	bwe-nas **tar**des
See you later	**Hasta luego**
	asta **lwe**-go
Please	**Por favor**
	por fa-**bor**
Don't mention it	**De nada**
	de **na**-da
With pleasure!	**¡Con mucho gusto!**
	ikon **moo**cho **goos**to!
Pardon?	**¿Cómo dice?**
	¿**ko**-mo **dee**the?
I'm sorry	**Lo siento**
	lo **syen**to
I don't know	**No sé**
	no se
Sir/Mr	**Señor/Sr.**
	se-**nyor**
Madam/Mrs/Ms	**Señora/Sra.**
	se-**nyo**-ra
Miss	**Señorita/Srta.**
	se-nyo-**ree**-ta
Excuse me!	**¡Oiga, por favor!**
(to catch attention)	i**oy**ga, por fa-**bor**!
Excuse me (sorry)	**Perdone**
	pair-**do**-ne

I don't understand	**No entiendo** no en-**tyen**-do
Do you understand?	**¿Entiende?** ¿en-**tyen**-de?
Do you speak English?	**¿Habla usted inglés?** ¿**a**-bla oos**ted** een**gles**?
I speak very little Spanish	**Hablo muy poco español** **a**-blo mwee **po**-ko es-pa-**nyol**
How are you?	**¿Cómo está?** ¿**ko**-mo es**ta**?
Fine, thanks	**Muy bien, gracias** mwee byen, **gra**-thyas
And you?	**¿Y usted?** ¿ee oos**ted**?

Key phrases

Asking for something in a shop or bar, you would ask for what you want, adding **por favor**.

the	**el/la/los/las** el/la/los/las
the museum	**el museo** el moo-**se**-o
the station	**la estación** la es-ta-**thyon**

13

the shops	**las tiendas**
	las **tyen**das
a/one (masc/fem)	**un/una**
	oon/**oo**na
a ticket	**un billete**
	oon bee-**lye**-te
one stamp	**un sello**
	oon **se**-lyo
a room	**una habitación**
	oona a-bee-ta-**thyon**
one bottle	**una botella**
	oona bo-**te**-lya
some (masculine)	**algún/alguno/algunos**
	al**goon**/al-**goo**-no/al-**goo**-nos
(feminine)	**alguna/algunas**
	al-**goo**-na/al-**goo**-nas
Would you like some bread?	**¿Quiere pan?**
	¿**kye**-re pan?
Have you got some coffee?	**¿Tiene café?**
	¿**tye**-ne ka-**fe**?
Do you have...?	**¿Tiene...?**
	¿**tye**-ne...?
Do you have a room?	**¿Tiene una habitación?**
	¿**tye**-ne **oo**na a-bee-ta-**thyon**?
I'd like...	**Querría...**
	ke-**rree**-a...
We'd like...	**Querríamos...**
	ke-**rree**-a-mos...

I'd like an ice cream	**Querría un helado**
	ke-**rree**-a oon e-**la**-do
We'd like to visit Toledo	**Querríamos visitar Toledo**
	ke-**rree**-a-mos bee-see-**tar** to-**le**-do
Some more bread?	**¿Más pan?**
	¿mas pan?
Some more soup?	**¿Más sopa?**
	¿mas **so**-pa?
Some more glasses?	**¿Más vasos?**
	¿mas **ba**-sos?
Another coffee	**Otro café**
	o-tro ka-**fe**
Another beer	**Otra cerveza**
	o-tra thair-**be**-tha
How much is it?	**¿Cuánto es?**
	¿**kwan**to es?
How much is the room?	**¿Cuánto cuesta la habitación?**
	¿**kwan**to **kwes**ta la a-bee-ta-**thyon**?
large/small	**grande/pequeño**
	grande/pe-**ke**-nyo
with/without	**con/sin**
	kon/seen
Where is...?	**¿Dónde está...?**
	¿**don**de es**ta**...?
Where are...?	**¿Dónde están...?**
	¿**don**de es**tan**...?

Where is the station?	**¿Dónde está la estación?**
	¿**don**de es**ta** la es-ta-**thyon**?
Where are the toilets?	**¿Dónde están los aseos?**
	¿**don**de es**tan** los a-**se**-os?
How do I get...?	**¿Cómo se va...?**
	¿**ko**-mo se ba...?
to the park	**al parque**
	al **par**ke
to the station	**a la estación**
	a la es-ta-**thyon**
to Madrid	**a Madrid**
	a ma-**dreed**
There is/are...	**Hay...**
	aee...
There isn't/ aren't any...	**No hay...**
	no **a**ee...
When...?	**¿Cuándo...?**
	¿**kwan**do...?
At what time...?	**¿A qué hora...?**
	¿a ke **o**-ra...?
today	**hoy**
	oy
tomorrow	**mañana**
	ma-**nya**-na
Can I smoke?	**¿Puedo fumar?**
	¿**pwe**-do foo**mar**?
Can I taste it?	**¿Puedo probarlo?**
	¿**pwe**-do pro-**bar**-lo?

How does this work?	**¿Cómo funciona?**
	¿**ko**-mo foon-**thyo**-na?
What does this mean?	**¿Qué significa?**
	¿ke seeg-nee-**fee**-ka?

Signs and notices

entrada	entrance
abierto	open
agua potable	drinking water
importe exacto	exact amount
no se admiten devoluciones	no refunds
no devuelve cambio	no change given
probadores	changing rooms
prohibido bañarse	no bathing
salida	exit
cerrado	closed
caliente	hot
frío	cold
caja	cash desk
autoservicio	self-service
tirar	pull
empujar	push
aseos	toilets
libre	vacant

ocupado	engaged
caballeros	gents
señoras	ladies
fuera de servicio	out of service
se aquila	for hire/to rent
se vende	for sale
rebajas	sale
sótano	basement
planta baja	ground floor
ascensor	lift
acceso a vías	to the trains
habitaciones libres	rooms available
salida de emergencia	emergency exit
completo	no vacancies
seleccione	choose
mañanas	mornings
tardes	afternoons
horario	timetable
llamar	ring
pulsar	press
billetes	tickets
salidas	departures
llegadas	arrivals
información	information
privado	private
no fumador	non-smoking
fumador	smoking
prohibido fumar	no smoking

Polite expressions

• •

There are two forms of address in Spanish: formal (**usted**) and informal (**tú**). You should always stick to the formal until you are invited to **tutear** (use the informal **tú**).

The meal/dinner was delicious	**La comida/cena estaba deliciosa** la ko-**mee**-da/**the**-na es-**ta**-ba de-lee-**thyo**-sa
This is a gift for you	**Esto es un regalo para ti/vosotros** **es**to es oon re-**ga**-lo pa-ra tee/ bo-**so**-tros
Thank you very much	**Muchas gracias** **moo**chas **gra**-thyas
Pleased to meet you	**Encantado(a)** en-kan-**ta**-do(a)
This is...	**Le presento a...** le pre-**sen**-to a...
my husband/wife	**mi marido/mujer** mee ma-**ree**-do/moo**khair**
Enjoy your holiday!	**¡Que disfrute(n) de sus vacaciones!** ike dees-**froo**-te(n) de soos ba-ka-**thyo**-nes!

19

Celebrations

• •

Traditional Christmas celebrations mainly take place on the night of **Nochebuena**, Christmas Eve. Presents are traditionally given on **los Reyes** or **el Día de Reyes** (6th January) but due to ever-increasing foreign influence some people also give presents on Christmas Day.

I'd like to wish you a...	**Le(Te) deseo que pase(s) un/unas...**
	le(te) de-**se**-o ke **pa**-se(s) oon/**oo**nas...
Happy Easter! / Merry Christmas!	**¡Felices Pascuas!/ ¡Feliz Navidad!**
	ife-**lee**-thes **pas**kwas!/ ife**leeth** na-bee-**dad**!
Happy New Year!	**¡Feliz Año (Nuevo)!**
	ife**leeth** a-nyo (**nwe**-bo)!
Happy birthday!	**¡Feliz cumpleaños!/ ¡Felicidades!**
	ife**leeth** koom-ple-**a**-nyos!/ ife-lee-thee-**da**-des!
Have a good trip!	**¡Buen viaje!**
	ibwen **bya**-khe!
Enjoy your meal!	**¡Que aproveche!**
	ike a-pro-**be**-che!

Making friends

●●

In this section we have used the informal **tú** for the
questions.

FACE TO FACE	
A	**¿Cómo te llamas?** ¿**ko**-mo te **lya**-mas? What's your name?
B	**Me llamo...** me **lya**-mo... My name is...
A	**¿De dónde eres?** ¿de **don**de **e**-res? Where are you from?
B	**Soy escocés(a), de Glasgow** soy es-ko-**the**-s(a), de **glas**gow I'm Scottish, from Glasgow
	Encantado(a) de conocerte(le) en-kan-**ta**-do(a) de ko-no-**thair**-te(le) Pleased to meet you

How old are you?	**¿Cuántos años tienes?** ¿**kwan**tos **a**-nyos **tye**-nes?
I'm ... years old	**Tengo ... años** **ten**go ... **a**-nyos
Where do you live?	**¿Dónde vives?** ¿**don**de **bee**bes?

21

Where do you live?	**¿Dónde vivís?**
(plural)	¿**don**de bee**bees**?
I live in London	**Vivo en Londres**
	¿**bee**bo en **lon**dres?
We live in Glasgow	**Vivimos en Glasgow**
	bee-**bee**-mos en **glas**gow
I'm still studying	**Todavía estoy estudiando**
	toda-**bee**-a es**toy** es-too-**dyan**-do
I work	**Trabajo**
	tra-**ba**-kho
I'm retired	**Estoy jubilado(a)**
	es**toy** khoo-bee-**la**-do(a)
I'm...	**Estoy...**
	es**toy**...
single	**soltero(a)**
	sol-**te**-ro(a)
married	**casado(a)**
	ka-**sa**-do(a)
divorced	**divorciado(a)**
	dee-bor-**thya**-do(a)
I have...	**Tengo...**
	tengo...
a boyfriend	**novio**
	no-byo
a girlfriend	**novia**
	no-bya
a partner	**pareja**
	pa-**re**-kha

I have ... children	**Tengo ... hijos**
	tengo ... **ee**khos
I have no children	**No tengo hijos**
	no **ten**go **ee**khos
I'm here...	**Estoy aquí...**
	es**toy** a-**kee**...
on holiday	**de vacaciones**
	de ba-ka-**thyo**-nes
for work	**por razones de trabajo**
	por ra-**tho**-nes de tra-**ba**-kho

Work

What work do you do?	**¿En qué trabaja?**
	¿en ke tra-**ba**-kha?
Do you enjoy it?	**¿Le gusta?**
	¿le **goo**sta?
I'm...	**Soy...**
	soy...
a doctor	**médico(a)**
	me-dee-ko(a)
a teacher	**profesor(a)**
	pro-fe-**sor**(a)
a secretary	**secretaria**
	se-kre-**ta**-rya
I'm self-employed	**Trabajo por cuenta propia**
	tra-**ba**-kho por **kwen**ta **pro**-pya

Weather

los chubascos los choo-**bas**-kos	showers
despejado des-pe-**kha**-do	clear
la lluvia la **lyoo**bya	rain
la niebla la **nye**-bla	fog
nublado noo-**bla**-do	cloudy

It's sunny	**Hace sol** **a**-the sol
It's raining	**Está lloviendo** es**ta** lyo-**byen**-do
It's snowing	**Está nevando** es**ta** ne-**ban**-do
It's windy	**Hace viento** **a**-the **byen**to
What a lovely day!	**¡Qué día más bueno!** ike **dee**-a mas **bwe**-no!
What awful weather!	**¡Qué tiempo tan malo!** ike **tyem**po tan **ma**-lo!
What will the weather be like tomorrow?	**¿Qué tiempo hará mañana?** ¿ke **tyem**po a-**ra** ma-**nya**-na?
Do you think it's going to rain?	**¿Cree que va a llover?** ¿**kre**-e ke ba a lyo-**bair**?

It's very hot	**Hace mucho calor**
	a-the **moo**cho ka-**lor**
Do you think there will be a storm?	**¿Cree que va a haber tormenta?**
	¿**kre**-e ke ba a a-**bair** tor-**men**-ta?
Do you think it will snow?	**¿Le parece que va a nevar?**
	¿le pa-**re**-the ke ba a ne-**bar**?
What is the temperature?	**¿Qué temperatura hace?**
	¿ke tem-pe-ra-**too**-ra **a**-the?

Getting around

Asking the way

enfrente (de) en-**fren**-te (de)	opposite (to)
al lado de al **la**-do de	next to
cerca de **thair**ka de	near to
el semáforo el se-**ma**-fo-ro	traffic lights
en la esquina en la es-**kee**-na	at the corner

FACE TO FACE

A **Oiga, señor/señora, ¿cómo se va a la estación?**

¿**oy**ga, se-**nyor**/se-**nyo**-ra, **ko**-mo se ba a la es-ta-**thyon**?

Excuse me, how do I get to the station?

B **Siga recto, después de la iglesia gire a la derecha/izquierda**

seega **rek**to, des**pwes** de la ee-**gle**-sya **khee**ere a la de-**re**-cha/eeth-**kyair**-da

Keep straight on, after the church turn right/left

26

A ¿Está lejos?
¿es**ta** le-khos?
Is it far?

B No, a doscientos metros/cinco minutos
no, a dos-**thyen**-tos **me**-tros/**theen**ko mee-**noo**-tos
No, 200 metres/five minutes

A Gracias!
gra-thyas!
Thank you!

B De nada
de **na**-da
You're welcome

We're looking for...	**Estamos buscando...**
	es-**ta**-mos boos-**kan**-do...
Is it far?	**¿Está lejos?**
	¿es**ta le**-khos?
Can I/we walk there?	**¿Se puede ir andando?**
	¿se **pwe**-de eer an-**dan**-do?
How do I/we get to the centre of (name of town)?	**¿Cómo se va al centro de...?**
	¿**ko**-mo se ba al **then**tro de...?
We're lost	**Nos hemos perdido**
	nos **e**-mos pair-**dee**-do
Can you show me where it is on the map?	**¿Puede indicarme dónde está en el mapa?**
	¿**pwe**-de een-dee-**kar**-me **don**de esta en el **ma**-pa?

YOU MAY HEAR...	
Después de pasar el puente des**pwes** de pa-**sar** el **pwen**te	After passing the bridge
Gire a la izquierda/ derecha **khee**re a la eeth-**kyair**-da/ de-**re**-cha	Turn left/right
Siga todo recto hasta llegar a... **see**ga **to**-do **rek**to **as**ta lye-**gar** a...	Keep straight on until you get to...

Bus and coach

● ●

A **bonobús** card is usually valid for 10 journeys and must be stamped on board the bus. The word for coach is **el autocar**.

FACE TO FACE

A **Oiga, ¿qué autobús va al centro?**
oyga, ¿ke ow-to-**boos** ba al **then**tro?
Excuse me, which bus goes to the centre?

B **El número quince**
el **noo**-me-ro **keen**the
Number fifteen

¿Dónde está la parada?
¿**don**de es**ta** la pa-**ra**-da?
Where is the bus stop?

Allí, a la derecha
a-**lyee,** a la de-**re**-cha
There, on the right

¿Dónde puedo comprar un bonobús?
¿**don**de **pwe**-do kom**prar** un bo-no-**boos**?
Where can I buy a bonobus card?

En el kiosko
en el kee-**os**-ko
At the news-stand

Is there a bus to...?	**¿Hay algún autobús que vaya a...?**
	¿**a**ee al**goon** ow-to-**boos** ke **ba**-ya a...?
Where do I catch the bus to...?	**¿Dónde se coge el autobús para...?**
	¿**don**de se **ko**-khe el ow-to-**boos** pa-ra...?
We're going to...	**Vamos a...**
	ba-mos a...
to the centre	**al centro**
	al **then**tro
to the beach	**a la playa**
	a la **pla**-ya

to the airport	**al aeropuerto**
	al a-e-ro-**pwair**-to
to Toledo	**a Toledo**
	a to-**le**-do
How often are the buses to...?	**¿Cada cuánto hay autobuses a...?**
	¿**ka**-da **kwan**tó a-ee ow-to-**boo**-ses a...?
When is the first/the last bus to...?	**¿Cuándo sale el primer/ el último autobús para...?**
	¿**kwan**do **sa**-le el pree**mair**/el **ool**-tee-mo ow-to-**boos** pa-ra...?
Please tell me when to get off	**Por favor, ¿me dice cuándo tengo que bajarme?**
	por fa-**bor**, ¿me **dee**the **kwan**do **ten**go ke ba-**khar**-me?
Please let me off	**¿Me deja salir, por favor?**
	¿me **de**-kha sa-**leer** por fa-**bor**?
This is my stop	**Me bajo en esta parada**
	me **ba**-kho en **es**ta pa-**ra**-da

YOU MAY HEAR...	
Este autobús no para en... **es**te ow-to-**boos** no **pa**-ra en...	This bus doesn't stop in...
Tiene que coger el... **tye**-ne ke ko-**khair** el...	You have to catch the...

30

Metro

•••••••••••••••••••••••••••••••••••••••

You can buy either **un metrobús**, which is valid for
10 journeys or **un abono de transporte**, which
covers a month's travel on both bus and metro.

la entrada	la en-**tra**-da	entrance
la salida	la sa-**lee**-da	way out/exit
el andén	el an**den**	metro line

Where is the nearest metro station?	**¿Dónde está la estación de metro más cercana?** ¿**don**de esta la es-ta-**thyon** de **me**-tro mas thair-**ka**-na?
I'm going to...	**Voy a...** boy a...
A metrobus ticket please	**Un metrobús, por favor** oon me-tro-**boos** por fa-**bor**
Do you have a map of the metro?	**¿Tiene un plano del metro?** ¿**tye**-ne oon **pla**-no del **me**-tro?
How do I/we get to...?	**¿Cómo se va a...?** ¿**ko**-mo se ba a...?
Do I have to change?	**¿Tengo que cambiar de línea?** ¿**ten**go ke kam**byar** de **lee**-ne-a?
What is the next stop?	**¿Cuál es la próxima parada?** ¿kwal es la **prok**-see-ma pa-**ra**-da?
Please let me through	**¿Me deja pasar, por favor?** ¿me **de**-kha pa-**sar**, por fa-**bor**?

> **Luggage** (p 94)

Train

There are three types of tickets on the high-speed AVE train – **Club**, **Preferente** and **Turista**. Prices vary according to time: **Punta** (peak), **Valle** (off-peak), and **Llano** (standard). A useful website is **www.renfe.es**

sencillo sen-**thee**-lyo	single/one-way
ida y vuelta	return
eeda ee **bwel**ta	
el horario el o-**ra**-ryo	timetable
salidas sa-**lee**-das	departures
llegadas lye-ga-das	arrivals
diario dee-**a**-ryo	daily

FACE TO FACE

A **¿A qué hora es el próximo tren para...?**
   ¿a ke **o**-ra es el **prok**-see-mo tren pa-ra...?
   When is the next train to...?

B **A las cinco y diez**
   a las **theen**ko ee dyeth
   At 17.10

Querría tres billetes, por favor
ke-**rree**-a tres bee-**lye**-tes, por fa-**bor**
I'd like three tickets, please
¿sencillos o de ida y vuelta?
¿sen-**thee**-lyos o de **ee**da ee **bwel**ta?
single or return?

Where is the station?	**¿Dónde está la estación?** ¿**don**de es**ta** la es-ta-**thyon**?
Two return tickets to...	**Dos billetes de ida y vuelta a...** dos bee-**lye**-tes de **ee**da ee **bwel**ta a...
A single to...	**Un billete de ida a...** oon bee-**lye**-te de **ee**da a...
Tourist class	**De clase turista** de **kla**-se too-**rees**-ta
Is there a supplement to pay?	**¿Hay que pagar suplemento?** ¿**a**ee ke pa-**gar** soo-ple-**men**-to?
I want to book a seat on the AVE to Seville	**Querría reservar un asiento en el AVE a Sevilla** ke-**rree**-a re-sair-**bar** oon a-**syen**-to en el **a**-be a se-**bee**-lya
When is the first/ last train to...?	**¿Cuándo es el primer/último tren para...?** ¿**kwan**do es el pree**mair**/ el **ool**-tee-mo tren pa-ra...?

Train

Do I have to change?	**¿Tengo que hacer transbordo?**
	¿**ten**go ke a-**thair** trans-**bor**-do?
Where?	**¿Dónde?**
	¿**don**de?
Which platform does it leave from?	**¿De qué andén sale?**
	¿de ke an**den sa**-le?
Is this the right platform for the train to...?	**¿Sale de este andén el tren para...?**
	¿**sa**-le de **es**te an**den** el tren pa-ra...?
Is this the train for...?	**¿Es este el tren para...?**
	¿es **es**te el tren pa-ra...?
When will it leave?	**¿Cuándo saldrá?**
	¿**kwan**do sal**dra**?
Does the train stop at...?	**¿Para el tren en...?**
	¿**pa**-ra el tren en...?
When does it arrive in...?	**¿Cuándo llega a...?**
	¿**kwan**do **lye**-ga a...?
Please let me know when we get to...	**Por favor, ¿me avisa cuando lleguemos a...?**
	por fa-**bor**, ¿me a-**bee**-sa **kwan**do lye-**ge**-mos a...?
Is there a buffet on the train?	**¿Hay servicio de cafetería en el tren?**
	¿**a**ee sair-**bee**-thyo de ka-fe-te-**ree**-a en el tren?
Is this free? (seat)	**¿Está libre?**
	¿es**ta lee**bre?
Excuse me	**¡Perdón!**
	¡pair**don**!

Taxi

• •

In most places taxis are plentiful, reliable and not
very expensive. Prices may often be displayed at the
taxi stand.

I need a taxi	**Necesito un taxi**
	ne-the-**see**-to oon **tak**see
Where is the taxi stand?	**¿Dónde está la parada de taxis?**
	¿**don**de es**ta** la pa-**ra**-da de **tak**sees?
Please order me a taxi	**Por favor, ¿me pide un taxi?**
	por fa-**bor**, ¿me **pee**de oon **tak**see?
straightaway	**enseguida**
	en-se-**gee**-da
for (time)	**para las...**
	pa-ra las...
How much is the taxi fare...?	**¿Cuánto cuesta ir en taxi...?**
	¿**kwan**to **kwes**ta eer en **tak**see...?
into town	**al centro**
	al **then**tro
to the hotel	**al hotel**
	al o-**tel**
to the station	**a la estación**
	a la es-ta-**thyon**
to the airport	**al aeropuerto**
	al a-e-ro-**pwair**-to

to this address	**a esta dirección**
	a **es**ta dee-rek-**thyon**
Please take me/ us to...	**Me/Nos lleva a ... por favor**
	me/nos **lye**-ba a ... por fa-**bor**
How much is it?	**¿Cuánto es?**
	¿**kwan**to es?
Why are you charging me so much?	**¿Cómo me cobra tanto?**
	¿**ko**-mo me **ko**-bra **tan**to?
It's more than on the meter	**Es más de lo que marca el taxímetro**
	es mas de lo ke **mar**ka el tak-**see**-me-tro
Keep the change	**Quédese con la vuelta**
	ke-de-se kon la **bwel**ta
Sorry, I don't have any change	**Lo siento, no tengo nada de cambio**
	lo **syen**to, no **ten**go **na**-da de **kam**byo
I'm in a hurry	**Tengo mucha prisa**
	tengo **moo**cha **pree**sa

Boat and ferry

la travesía	la tra-be-**see**-a	crossing
el crucero	el kroo-**the**-ro	cruise
el camarote		cabin
el ka-ma-**ro**-te		

When is the next boat/ferry to...?	**¿Cuándo sale el próximo barco/ferry para...?**
	¿**kwan**do **sa**-le el **prok**-see-mo **bar**ko/ferry pa-ra...?
Have you a timetable?	**¿Tienen un horario?**
	¿**tye**-nen oon o-**ra**-ryo?
Is there a car ferry to...?	**¿Hay ferry para coches a...?**
	¿aee **fe**rry pa-ra **ko**-ches a?
How much is a ticket...?	**¿Cuánto cuesta el billete...?**
	¿**kwan**to **kwes**ta el bee-**lye**-te...?
single	**sencillo/de ida**
	sen-**thee**-lyo/de **ee**da
return	**de ida y vuelta**
	de **ee**da ee **bwel**ta
A tourist ticket	**Un billete de clase turista**
	oon bee-**lye**-te de **kla**-se too-**rees**-ta
How much is the crossing for a car and ... people?	**¿Cuánto cuesta un pasaje para ... personas y un coche?**
	¿**kwan**to **kwes**ta oon pa-**sa**-khe pa-ra ... pair-**so**-nas ee oon **ko**-che?
How long is the journey?	**¿Cuánto dura el viaje?**
	¿**kwan**to **doo**ra el **bya**-khe?
What time do we get to...?	**¿A qué hora llegamos a...?**
	¿a ke **o**-ra lye-**ga**-mos a...?
Where does the boat leave from?	**¿De dónde sale el barco?**
	¿de **don**de **sa**-le el **bar**ko?

| When is the first/
the last boat? | ¿Cuándo sale el primer/
el último barco?
¿**kwan**do **sa**-le el pree**mair**/
el **ool**-tee-mo **bar**ko? |
| Is there
somewhere to
eat on the boat? | ¿Hay cafetería/restaurante
en el barco?
¿**a**ee ka-fe-te-**ree**-a/res-tow-
ran-te en el **bar**ko? |

Air travel

....

How do I get to the airport?	¿Cómo se va al aeropuerto? ¿**ko**-mo se ba al a-e-ro-**pwair**-to?
To the airport, please	Al aeropuerto, por favor al a-e-ro-**pwair**-to, por fa-**bor**
I have to catch...	Tengo que coger... **ten**go ke kho-**khair**...
the ... o'clock flight to...	el vuelo de las ... para... el **bwe**-lo de las ... pa-ra...
Is there a bus to the airport?	¿Hay algún autobús al aeropuerto? ¿**a**ee al**goon** ow-to-**boos** al a-e-ro-**pwair**-to?
How do I/we get to the centre of (name of town)?	¿Cómo se va al centro de...? ¿**ko**-mo se ba al **then**tro de...?

38

Is there a bus to the city centre?	**¿Hay algún autobús que vaya al centro?**
	¿**a**ee al**goon** ow-to-**boos** ke **ba**-ya al **then**tro?
Where is the luggage for the flight from...?	**¿Dónde está el equipaje del vuelo de...?**
	¿**don**de es**ta** el e-kee-pa-khe del **bwe**-lo de...?

YOU MAY HEAR...

El embarque se efectuará por la puerta número... el em-**bar**-ke se e-fek-twa-**ra** por la **pwair**ta **noo**-me-ro...	Boarding will take place at gate number...
Última llamada para los pasajeros del vuelo... ool-tee-ma lya-**ma**-da pa-ra los pa-sa-**khe**-ros del **bwe**-lo...	Last call for passengers on flight number...
Su vuelo sale con retraso soo **bwe**-lo **sa**-le kon re-**tra**-so	Your flight is delayed

Customs control

• •

With the single European Market, European Union (EU) citizens are subject only to highly selective spot checks and they can go through the blue customs channel when arriving from another EU country.

UE oo eh	EU
la aduana la a-doo-**a**-na	customs control
el pasaporte el pa-sa-**por**-te	passport

Do I have to pay duty on this?	**¿Tengo que pagar derechos de aduana por esto?** ¿**ten**go ke pa**gar** de-**re**-chos de a-doo-**a**-na por **es**to?
It is for my own personal use	**Es para uso personal** es pa-ra **oo**so pair-so-**nal**
We are on our way to... (if in transit through a country)	**Estamos aquí de paso.** **Vamos a...** es-**ta**-mos a-**kee** de pa-so. **ba**-mos a...

Driving

Car hire

el permiso de conducir el pair-**mee**-so de kon-doo-**theer**	driving licence
el seguro el se-**goo**-ro	insurance
la marcha atrás la **mar**cha a-**tras**	reverse gear

I want to hire a car	**Querría alquilar un coche** ke-**rree**-a al-kee-**lar** oon **ko**-che
for ... days/the weekend	**para ... días/el fin de semana** pa-ra ... **dee**as/el feen de se-**ma**-na
What are your rates...?	**¿Qué tarifas tienen...?** ¿ke ta-**ree**-fas **tye**-nen...?
per day	**por día** por **dee**a
per week	**por semana** por se-**ma**-na
How much is the deposit?	**¿Cuánto hay que dejar de depósito?** ¿**kwan**to **a**ee ke de-**khar** de de-**po**-see-to?

41

Is there a mileage (km) charge?	**¿Hay que pagar kilometraje?**
	¿**a**ee ke pa-**gar** kee-lo-me-**tra**-khe?
How much?	**¿Cuánto?**
	¿**kwan**to?
Is fully comprehensive insurance included in the price?	**¿El seguro a todo riesgo va incluido en el precio?**
	¿el se-**goo**-ro a **to**-do **ryes**go ba een-kloo-**ee**-do en el **pre**-thyo?
Do I have to return the car here?	**¿Tengo que devolver el coche aquí mismo?**
	¿**ten**go ke de-bol-**bair** el **ko**-che a-**kee mees**mo?
By what time?	**¿Para qué hora?**
	¿pa-ra ke **o**-ra?
I'd like to leave it in...	**Quisiera dejarlo en...**
	kee-**sye**-ra de-**khar**-lo en...
Can you show me how the controls work?	**¿Me enseña cómo funcionan los mandos?**
	¿me en-**se**-nya **ko**-mo foon-**thyo**-nan los **man**dos?

YOU MAY HEAR...

Por favor, devuelva el coche con el depósito lleno por fa-**bor**, de-**bwel**ba el **ko**-che kon el de-**po**-see-to **lye**-no	Please return the car with a full tank

Driving

• •

The speed limits in Spain are 50 km/h in built-up
areas, 90 km/h on ordinary roads and 120 km/h
on **autovías** (dual carriageways) and **autopistas**
(motorways). Some motorways are toll paying
(**peaje**). Payment is due on completion of each
section. A useful website for motorway information
is **www.aseta.es**

Can I/we park here?	**¿Se puede aparcar aquí?**
	¿se **pwe**-de a-par-**kar** a-**kee**?
How long can I/we park for here?	**¿Cuánto tiempo se puede aparcar aquí?**
	¿**kwan**to **tyem**po se **pwe**-de a-par-**kar** a-**kee**?
How do I/we get to the motorway?	**¿Por dónde se va a la autopista?**
	¿por **don**de se ba a la ow-to-**pee**-sta?
Which junction is it for...?	**¿Cuál es la salida de...?**
	¿kwal es la sa-**lee**-da de...?
Do I/we need snow chains?	**¿Hace falta usar cadenas?**
	¿**a**-the **fal**ta oo**sar** ka-**de**-nas?

Petrol

●●●●●●●●●●●●●●●●●●●●●●●●●●●●●●●●●●●●●●

Unleaded petrol pumps are always coloured green.

sin plomo seen **plo**-mo	unleaded
gasoil/gasóleo ga-**soyl**/ga-**so**-le-o	diesel
el surtidor el soor-tee-**dor**	petrol pump

Is there a petrol station near here?	**¿Hay una estación de servicio por aquí cerca?** ¿**a**ee **oo**na es-ta-**thyon** de sair-**bee**-thyo por a-**kee thair**ka?
Fill it up, please	**Lleno, por favor** **lye**-no, por fa-**bor**
Can you check the oil/the water?	**¿Me revisa el aceite/el agua?** ¿me re-**bee**-sa el a-**the**-ee-te/el **a**-gwa?
...euros worth of unleaded petrol	**...euros de gasolina sin plomo** ...**eoo**-ros de ga-so-**lee**-na seen **plo**-mo
Where is...?	**¿Dónde está...?** ¿**don**de es**ta**...?
the air	**el aire** el **aee**-re
the water	**el agua** el **a**-gwa

Can you check the tyre pressure, please?	¿Me revisa la presión de los neumáticos, por favor?
	¿me re-**bee**-sa la pre-**syon** de los neoo-**ma**-tee-kos, por fa-**bor**?
Can I pay with this credit card?	¿Puedo pagar con esta tarjeta de crédito?
	¿**pwe**-do pa-**gar** kon **es**ta tar-**khe**-ta de **kre**-dee-to?

YOU MAY HEAR...

| ¿Qué surtidor ha usado? | Which pump did you use? |
| ¿ke soor-tee-**dor** a oo-**sa**-do? | |

Breakdown

Can you help me?	¿Puede ayudarme?
	¿**pwe**-de a-yoo-**dar**-me?
My car has broken down	Se me ha averiado el coche
	se me a a-be-**rya**-do el **ko**-che
I've run out of petrol	Me he quedado sin gasolina
	me e ke-**da**-do seen ga-so-**lee**-na
Is there a garage near here?	¿Hay un taller por aquí cerca?
	¿**a**ee oon ta-**lyair** por a-**kee thair**ka?
I've got a flat tyre	Tengo una rueda pinchada
	tengo **oo**na **rwe**-da peen-**cha**-da

45

Do you have parts for a (make of car)?	**¿Tiene repuestos para el...?** ¿**tye**-ne re-**pwes**-tos pa-ra el...?
The ... doesn't work properly (see car parts)	**El/La ... no funciona bien** el/la ... no foon-**thyo**-na byen
Can you replace ....?	**¿Me puede cambiar ....?** ¿me **pwe**-de kam**byar**?

Car parts

• •

The ... doesn't work	**El/La ... no funciona** el/la ... no foon-**thyo**-na
The ... don't work	**Los/Las ... no funcionan** los/las ... no foon-**thyo**-nan

accelerator	**el acelerador**	a-the-le-ra-**dor**
battery	**la batería**	ba-te-**ree**-a
bonnet	**el capó**	ka-**po**
brakes	**los frenos**	**fre**-nos
choke	**el estárter**	es-**tar**-tair
clutch	**el embrague**	em-**bra**-ge
distributor	**el distribuidor**	dees-tree-bwee-**dor**
engine	**el motor**	mo-**tor**
exhaust pipe	**el tubo de escape**	**too**bo de es-**ka**-pe
fuse	**el fusible**	foo-**see**-ble

46

gears	las marchas	**mar**chas
handbrake	el freno de mano	**fre**-no de **ma**-no
headlights	los faros	**fa**-ros
ignition	el encendido	en-then-**dee**-do
indicator	el intermitente	een-tair-mee-**ten**-te
points	los platinos	pla-**tee**-nos
radiator	el radiador	ra-dya-**dor**
rear lights	los pilotos	pee-**lo**-tos
seat belt	el cinturón de seguridad	theen-too-**ron** de se-goo-ree-**dad**
spare wheel	la rueda de repuesto	**rwe**-da de re-**pwes**-to
spark plugs	las bujías	boo-**khee**-as
steering	la dirección	dee-rek-**thyon**
steering wheel	el volante	bo-**lan**-te
tyre	el neumático	neoo-**ma**-tee-ko
wheel	la rueda	**rwe**-da
windscreen	el parabrisas	pa-ra-**bree**-sas
windscreen washer	el lavaparabrisas	la-ba-pa-ra-**bree**-sas
windscreen wiper	el limpiaparabrisas	leem-pya-pa-ra-**bree**-sas

Road signs

PELIGRO
danger

CURVAS
PELIGROSAS

dangerous bends

libre
spaces

completo
full

CEDA EL PASO
give way

Norte

Oeste

Este

Sur

NO APARCAR

no parking

NO ESTACIONAR

no stopping

SENTIDO ÚNICO

one way

end of right of way

AUTOVÍA

dual carriageway

AUTOPISTA

motorway

Staying somewhere

Hotel (booking)

••••••••••••••••••••••••••••••••••

FACE TO FACE

A **Querría reservar una habitación individual/doble**

ke-**rree**-a re-sair-**bar oo**na a-bee-ta-**thyon** een-dee-bee-**dwal**/**do**-ble

I'd like to book a single/double room

B **¿Para cuántas noches?**

¿pa-ra **kwan**tas **no**-ches?

For how many nights?

A **Para una noche/... noches ; del ... al ...**

pa-ra **oo**na **no**-che/... **no**-ches ; del ... al ...

For one night/... nights ; from ... till ...

Do you have a room for tonight?	**¿Tiene una habitación para esta noche?** ¿**tye**-ne **oo**na a-bee-ta-**thyon** pa-ra **es**ta **no**-che?

50

double	**doble**
	do-ble
single	**individual**
	een-dee-bee-**dwal**
with bath	**con baño**
	kon **ba**nyo
with shower	**con ducha**
	kon **doo**cha
with a double bed	**con cama de matrimonio**
	kon **ka**-ma de ma-tree-**mo**-nyo
twin-bedded	**con dos camas**
	kon dos **ka**-mas
How much is it...?	**¿Qué precio tiene...?**
	¿ke **pre**-thyo **tye**-ne...?
per night	**por noche**
	por **no**-che
per week	**por semana**
	por se-**ma**-na
for half board	**con media pensión**
	kon **me**-dya pen**syon**
full board	**con pensión completa**
	kon pen**syon** kom-**ple**-ta
with breakfast	**con desayuno**
	kon de-sa-**yoo**-no
Is breakfast included?	**¿Está incluido el desayuno?**
	¿es**ta** een-kloo-**ee**-do el de-sa-**yoo**-no?

| Is there room service? | **¿Hay servicio de habitaciones?** ¿**a**ee sair-**bee**-thyo de a-bee-ta-**thyo**-nes? |
| Can I see the room? | **¿Puedo ver la habitación?** ¿**pwe**-do bair la a-bee-ta-**thyon**? |

YOU MAY HEAR...	
Está todo ocupado es**ta to**-do o-koo-**pa**-do	We're full
¿Para cuántas noches? ¿pa-ra **kwan**tas **no**-ches?	For how many nights?
¿Su nombre, por favor? ¿soo **nom**bre, por fa-**bor**?	Your name, please?
Por favor confírmelo... por fa-**bor** kon-**feer**-me-lo...	Please confirm...
por escrito por es-**kree**-to	by letter
por fax por faks	by fax

Hotel desk

• •

You may be required to fill in a registration form and give your passport number.

I booked a room...	**Tengo una habitación reservada...** **ten**go **oo**na a-bee-ta-**thyon** re-sair-**ba**-da...
in the name of...	**a nombre de...** a **nom**bre de...
Where can I park the car?	**¿Dónde puedo aparcar el coche?** ¿**don**de **pwe**-do a-par-**kar** el **ko**-che?
What time is...?	**¿A qué hora es...?** ¿a ke **o**-ra es...?
dinner	**la cena** la **the**-na
breakfast	**el desayuno** el de-sa-**yoo**-no
The key for room number...	**¿Me da la llave de la habitación...?** ¿me da la **lya**-be de la a-bee-ta-**thyon**...?
I'm leaving tomorrow	**Me voy mañana** me boy ma-**nya**-na
Please prepare the bill	**¿Me prepara la cuenta, por favor?** ¿me pre-**pa**-ra la **kwen**ta, por fa-**bor**?

Camping

Local tourist offices should have **una guía de campings** with prices.

How far is the beach?	**¿A qué distancia está la playa?**
	¿a ke dees-**tan**-thya es**ta** la **pla**-ya?
Is there a restaurant on the campsite?	**¿Hay restaurante en el camping?**
	¿**a**ee res-tow-**ran**-te en el **kam**peen?
Do you have any vacancies?	**¿Tienen plazas libres?**
	¿**tye**-nen **pla**-thas **lee**bres?
Is hot water included in the price?	**¿El agua caliente va incluida en el precio?**
	¿el **a**-gwa ka-**lyen**-te ba een-kloo-**ee**-da en el **pre**-thyo?
We'd like to stay for ... nights	**Quisiéramos quedarnos... noches**
	kee-**sye**-ra-mos ke-**dar**-nos ... **no**-ches
How much is it per night...?	**¿Cuánto cuesta por noche...?**
	¿**kwan**to **kwes**ta por **no**-che...?
for a tent	**por tienda**
	por **tyen**da
per person	**por persona**
	por pair-**so**-na

Self-catering

●●

If you arrive with no accommodation and want
to go self-catering, look for signs **Alquiler de
Apartamentos** (apartments for rent).

Who do we contact if there are problems?	**¿A quién avisamos si hay algún problema?**
	¿a kyen a-bee-**sa**-mos see **a**ee al**goon** pro-**ble**-ma?
How does the heating work?	**¿Cómo funciona la calefacción?**
	¿**ko**-mo foon-**thyo**-na la ka-le-fak-**thyon**?
Where is the nearest supermarket?	**¿Dónde está el supermercado más cercano?**
	¿**don**de es**ta** el soo-pair-mair-**ka**-do mas thair-**ka**-no?
Where do we leave the rubbish?	**¿Dónde se deja la basura?**
	¿**don**de se **de**-kha la ba-**soo**-ra?

> **Sightseeing and tourist office** (p 69)

Shopping

Shopping phrases

Most shops close for lunch approx. 1.30 to 5.00 or 5.30 pm and stay open till about 8.30 pm. Department stores remain open all day.

YOU MAY HEAR...	
¿Qué desea? ¿ke de-**se**-a?	Can I help you?
¿Tiene...? ¿**tye**-ne...?	Do you have...?
Por supuesto, aquí tiene por soo-**pwes**-to, a-**kee tye**-ne	Certainly, here you are
¿Algo más? ¿**al**go mas?	Anything else?

Where is...?	**¿Dónde está...?** ¿**don**de es**ta**?
Where can I buy...?	**¿Dónde puedo comprar...?** ¿**don**de **pwe**-do kom**prar**...?

toys	**juguetes**
	khoo-**ge**-tes
gifts	**regalos**
	re-**ga**-los
I'm looking for a present for...	**Estoy buscando un regalo para...**
	es**toy** boos-**kan**-do oon re-**ga**-lo pa-ra...
my mother	**mi madre**
	mee **ma**-dre
a child	**un niño**
	oon **neen**yo
Which floor are shoes on?	**¿En qué planta están los zapatos?**
	¿en ke **plan**ta es**tan** los tha-**pa**-tos?
Where is the lingerie department?	**¿Dónde está la sección de lencería?**
	¿**don**de es**ta** la sek**thyon** de len-the-**ree**-a?
It's too expensive for me	**Me resulta demasiado caro**
	me re-**sool**-ta de-ma-**sya**-do **ka**-ro
Have you anything else?	**¿No tiene otra cosa?**
	¿no **tye**-ne **o**-tra **ko**-sa?

57

Shops

....

liquidación/rebajas lee-kee-da-**thyon/** re-**ba**-khas	sale/reductions
hoy abierto hasta las... hoy a-**byair**-to **as**ta las...	open today till...

baker's	**panadería**	pa-na-de-**ree**-a
butcher's	**carnicería**	kar-nee-the-**ree**-a
cake shop	**pastelería/** **confitería**	pas-te-le-**ree**-a/ kon-fee-te-**ree**-a
clothes (women's)	**ropa de señora**	**ro**-pa de se-**nyo**-ra
clothes (men's)	**ropa de caballero**	**ro**-pa de ka-ba-**lye**-ro
clothes (children's)	**ropa de niños**	**ro**-pa de **neen**yos
fishmonger's	**pescadería**	pes-ka-de-**ree**-a
gifts	**regalos**	re-**ga**-los
greengrocer's	**frutería**	froo-te-**ree**-a
grocer's	**tienda de comestibles**	**tyen**da de ko-mes-**tee**-bles
hairdresser's	**peluquería**	pe-loo-ke-**ree**-a
jeweller's	**joyería**	kho-ye-**ree**-a
pharmacy	**farmacia**	far-**ma**-thya
shoe shop	**zapatería**	tha-pa-te-**ree**-a
sports	**deportes**	de-**por**-tes

supermarket	**supermercado**	soo-pair-mair-**ka**-do
tobacconist's	**estanco**	es-**tan**-ko
toys	**juguetes**	khoo-**ge**-tes

Food (general)

biscuits	**las galletas**	ga-**lye**-tas
bread	**el pan**	pan
bread (wholemeal)	**el pan integral**	pan een-te-**gral**
bread roll	**el panecillo**	pa-ne-**thee**-lyo
butter	**la mantequilla**	man-te-**kee**-lya
cereal	**los cereales**	the-re-**a**-les
cheese	**el queso**	**ke**-so
chicken	**el pollo**	**po**-lyo
coffee (instant)	**el café (instantáneo)**	ka-**fe** (eens-tan-**ta**-ne-o)
cream	**la nata**	**na**-ta
crisps	**las patatas fritas**	pa-**ta**-tas **free**-tas
eggs	**los huevos**	**we**-bos
flour	**la harina**	a-**ree**-na
ham (cooked)	**el jamón (de) York**	kha-**mon** (de) york
ham (cured)	**el jamón serrano**	kha-**mon** se-**rra**-no

herbal tea	la infusión	een-foo-**syon**
honey	la miel	myel
jam	la mermelada	mair-me-**la**-da
margarine	la margarina	mar-ga-**ree**-na
marmalade	la mermelada de naranja	mair-me-**la**-da de na-**ran**-kha
milk	la leche	**le**-che
mustard	la mostaza	mos-**ta**-tha
olive oil	el aceite de oliva	a-**they**-te de o-**lee**-ba
orange juice	el zumo de naranja	**thoo**mo de na-**ran**-kha
pepper	la pimienta	pee-**myen**-ta
rice	el arroz	a-**rroth**
salt	la sal	sal
stock cube	el cubito de caldo	koo-**bee**-to de **kal**do
sugar	el azúcar	a-**thoo**-kar
tea	el té	te
tin of tomatoes	la lata de tomate	**la**-ta de to-**ma**-te
vinegar	el vinagre	bee-**na**-gre
yoghurt	el yogur	yo-**goor**

 > **Measurements and quantities** (p 115)

Food (fruit and veg)

Fruit

apples	**las manzanas**	man-**tha**-nas
apricots	**los albaricoques**	al-ba-ree-**ko**-kes
bananas	**los plátanos**	**pla**-ta-nos
cherries	**las cerezas**	the-**re**-thas
grapefruit	**el pomelo**	po-**me**-lo
grapes	**las uvas**	**oo**bas
lemon	**el limón**	lee**mon**
melon	**el melón**	me-**lon**
nectarines	**las nectarinas**	nek-ta-**ree**-nas
oranges	**las naranjas**	na-**ran**-khas
peaches	**los melocotones**	me-lo-ko-**to**-nes
pears	**las peras**	**pe**-ras
pineapple	**la piña**	**peen**ya
plums	**las ciruelas**	thee-**rwe**-las
raspberries	**las frambuesas**	fram-**bwe**-sas
strawberries	**las fresas**	**fre**-sas
watermelon	**la sandía**	san-**dee**-a

Vegetables

asparagus	**los espárragos**	es-**pa**-rra-gos
carrots	**las zanahorias**	tha-na-**o**-ryas

cauliflower	la coliflor	ko-lee-**flor**
courgettes	los calabacines	ka-la-ba-**thee**-nes
French beans	las judías verdes	khoo-**dee**-as **bair**des
garlic	el ajo	**a**-kho
leeks	los puerros	**pwe**rros
lettuce	la lechuga	le-**choo**ga
mushrooms	los champiñones	cham-pee-**nyo**-nes
onions	las cebollas	the-**bo**-lyas
peas	los guisantes	gee-**san**-tes
peppers	los pimientos	pee-**myen**-tos
potatoes	las patatas	pa-**ta**-tas
spinach	las espinacas	es-pee-**na**-kas
tomatoes	los tomates	to-**ma**-tes

Clothes

....

women's sizes		men's suit sizes		shoe sizes			
UK	EU	UK	EU	UK	EU	UK	EU
8	36	36	46	2	35	7	41
10	38	38	48	3	36	8	42
12	40	40	50	4	37	9	43
14	42	42	52	5	38	10	44
16	44	44	54	6	39	11	45
18	46	46	56				

¿Puedo probarmelo?
¿**pwe**-do pro-**bar**-me-lo?
May I try this on?

Sí, los probadores están allí
see, los pro-ba-**do**-res es**tan** a-**lyee**
Yes, the changing rooms are over there

**¿Tiene una talla pequeña/mediana/grande/
extra grande?**
¿**tye**-ne **oo**na **ta**-lya pe-**ke**-nya/me-**dya**-na/
grande/**eks**tra **gran**de?
Do you have a small/medium/large/extra large
size?

Sólo tenemos esta talla en este color
so-lo te-**ne**-mos **es**ta **ta**-lya en **es**te co-**lor**
In this colour we only have this size

Where are the changing rooms?	**¿Dónde están los probadores?**
	¿**don**de es**tan** los pro-ba-**do**-res?
I take size 42 (clothes)	**Uso la cuarenta y dos**
	ooso la kwa-**ren**-ta ee **dos**
I take size 39 (shoes)	**Uso el treinta y nueve**
	ooso el **treyn**ta ee **nwe**-be
I'd like to return...	**Quiero devolver...**
	kye-ro de-bol-**bair**...
Can I have my money back?	**¿Me devuelven el dinero?**
	¿me de-**bwel**-ben el dee-**ne**-ro?

I'm just looking	**Solo estoy mirando**
	so-lo es**toy** mee-**ran**-do
I'll take it	**Me lo llevo**
	me lo **lye**-vo

Clothes (articles)

• •

belt	**el cinturón**	theen-too-**ron**
blouse	**la blusa**	**bloo**sa
bra	**el sujetador**	soo-khe-ta-**dor**
coat	**el abrigo**	a-**bree**-go
dress	**el vestido**	bes-**tee**-do
gloves	**los guantes**	**gwan**tes
hat	**el sombrero**	som-**bre**-ro
hat (woollen)	**el gorro**	**go**-rro
jacket	**la chaqueta**	cha-**ke**-ta
jeans	**los vaqueros**	ba-**ke**-ros
knickers	**las bragas**	**bra**-gas
nightdress	**el camisón**	ka-mee-**son**
pyjamas	**el pijama**	pee-**kha**-ma
raincoat	**el chubasquero**	choo-bas-**ke**-ro
sandals	**las sandalias**	san-**da**-lyas
scarf (silk)	**el pañuelo**	pa-**nwe**-lo
scarf (wool)	**la bufanda**	boo-**fan**-da
shirt	**la camisa**	ka-**mee**-sa

Shopping

> **Paying** (p 93) > **Numbers** (p 117)

shorts	**los pantalones cortos**	pan-ta-**lo**-nes **kor**tos
skirt	**la falda**	**fal**da
slippers	**las zapatillas**	tha-pa-**tee**-lyas
socks	**los calcetines**	kal-the-**tee**-nes
suit	**el traje**	**tra**-khe
swimsuit	**el traje de baño/ el bañador**	**tra**-khe de **ba**nyo/ba-nya-**dor**
tie	**la corbata**	kor-**ba**-ta
tights	**las medias**	**me**-dyas
tracksuit	**el chándal**	**chan**-dal
trousers	**los pantalones**	pan-ta-**lo**-nes
t-shirt	**la camiseta**	ka-mee-**se**-ta
underpants	**los calzoncillos**	kal-thon-**thee**-lyos
zip	**la cremallera**	kre-ma-**lye**-ra

Maps and guides

● ●

Have you...?	**¿Tiene...?**	¿**tye**-ne...?
a map of (name of town)	**un plano de...**	oon **pla**-no de...
a map of the region	**un mapa de la zona**	oon **ma**-pa de la **tho**-na

Can you show me where ... is on the map?	¿**Puede indicarme en el mapa dónde está...?**
	¿**pwe**-de een-dee-**kar**-me en el **ma**-pa **don**de esta...?
Do you have a guide book/a leaflet in English?	¿**Tiene alguna guía/algún folleto en inglés?**
	¿**tye**-ne al-**goo**-na **gee**-a/ al**goon** fo-**lye**-to en een**gles**?
Where can I/we buy an English newspaper/ magazine?	¿**Dónde se pueden comprar periódicos ingleses/revistas inglesas?**
	¿**don**de se **pwe**-den kom**prar** pe-ree-**o**-dee-kos een-**gle**-ses/ re-**bis**-tas een-**gle**-sas?

Post office

Generally open from 8.30 am to 8.30 pm Monday to Friday and from 9.30 am to 2 pm on Saturdays. Opening times can be checked at **www.correo.es**.

(la oficina de) correos (la o-fee-**thee**-na de) ko-**rre**-os	post office
el buzón el boo**thon**	postbox
los sellos los **se**-lyos	stamps

> **Asking the way** (p 26)

Is there a post office near here?	**¿Hay una oficina de Correos por aquí cerca?**
	¿**a**ee oon o-fee-**thee**-na de ko-**rre**-os por a-**kee thair**ka?
Do you sell stamps?	**¿Venden sellos?**
	¿**ben**den se-lyos?
Can I have stamps for ... postcards to Great Britain	**Me da sellos para ... postales para Gran Bretaña**
	¿me da **se**-lyos pa-ra ... pos-**ta**-les pa-ra gran bre-**ta**-nya?
How much is it to send this parcel?	**¿Cuánto cuesta mandar este paquete?**
	¿**kwan**to **kwes**ta man**dar es**te pa-**ke**-te?
How long will it take?	**¿Cuánto tarda en llegar?**
	¿**kwan**to **tar**da en lye-**gar**?
by air/by priority post/by registered post	**por avión/por correo urgente/ por correo certificado**
	por a-**byon**/por ko-**rre**-o oor-**khen**-te/por ko-**rre**-o thair-tee-fee-**ka**-do

YOU MAY HEAR...

| **Rellene este impreso** | Fill in this form |
| re-**lye**-ne **es**te eem-**pre**-so | |

> **Money** (p 91) > **Paying** (p 93)

Photos

●●●●●●●●●●●●●●●●●●●●●●●●●●●●●●●●●●●●●●

You can usually get good prices in specialist photographic shops, particularly for camcorder equipment.

A video tape for this camcorder	**Una cinta para esta videocámara** **oo**na **theen**ta pa-ra **es**ta bee-de-o-**ka**-ma-ra
A memory card for this digital camera	**Una tarjeta de memoria para esta cámara digital** **oo**na tar-**khe**-ta de me-**mo**-ree-a pa-ra **es**ta **ka**-ma-ra dee-khee-**tal**
Have you batteries...?	**¿Tiene pilas...?** ¿**tye**-ne **pee**las...?
for this camera/ this camcorder	**para esta cámara/esta videocámara** pa-ra **es**ta **ka**-ma-ra/esta bee-de-o-**ka**-ma-ra
Is it OK to take pictures here?	**¿Se pueden hacer fotos aquí?** ¿se **pwe**-den a-**thair fo**-tos a-**kee**?
Would you take a picture of us, please?	**¿Podría hacernos una foto, por favor?** ¿po-**dree**-a a-**thair**-nos oona **fo**-to, por fa-**bor**?

Leisure

Sightseeing and tourist office

The tourist office is called **la oficina de turismo**. If you are looking for somewhere to stay they should have details of hotels, campsites, etc. They also have free maps. Monday is not a good day for visiting museums, as this is the day they are generally closed.

Where is the tourist office?	**¿Dónde está la oficina de turismo?**
	¿**don**de es**ta** la o-fee-**thee**-na de too-**rees**-mo?
What can we visit in the area?	**¿Qué podemos visitar en la zona?**
	¿ke po-**de**-mos bee-see-**tar** en la **tho**-na?
Have you any leaflets?	**¿Tiene algún folleto?**
	¿**tye**-ne al**goon** fo-**lye**-to?

69

Are there any excursions?	¿Hay alguna excursión organizada?
	¿**a**ee al-**goo**-na eks-koor-**syon** or-ga-nee-**tha**-da?
We'd like to go to...	Nos gustaría ir a...
	nos goos-ta-**ree**-a eer a...
How much does it cost to get in?	¿Cuánto cuesta entrar?
	¿**kwan**to **kwes**ta en**trar**?
Are there any reductions for...?	¿Hacen descuento a...?
	¿**a**-then des-**kwen**-to a...?
children	los niños
	los **nee**-nyos
students	los estudiantes
	los es-too-**dyan**-tes
unemployed	los parados
	los pa-**ra**-dos
senior citizens	los jubilados
	los khoo-bee-**la**-dos
over 60s	mayores de sesenta
	ma-**yo**-res de se-**sen**-ta

> **Maps and guides** (p 65)

Entertainment

• •

In large cities you can often find **La Guía del Ocio**,
a magazine listing events and entertainment.
Newspapers usually carry a page called **Agenda
cultural** with local events.

What is there to do in the evenings?	**¿Qué se puede hacer por las noches?**
	¿ke se **pwe**-de a-**thair** por las **no**-ches?
Is there anything for children?	**¿Hay algo para los niños?**
	¿**a**ee **al**go **pa**-ra los **neen**yos?
I'd like ... tickets	**Quisiera ... entradas**
	kee-**sye**-ra ... en-**tra**-das
...adults	...**para mayores**
	...pa-ra ma-**yo**-res
...children	...**para niños**
	...pa-ra **neen**yos

YOU MAY HEAR...

La entrada cuesta ... euros con (derecho a) consumición	It costs ... euros to get in including a free drink
la en-**tra**-da **kwes**ta ... **eoo**-ros kon (de-**re**-cho a) kon-soo-mee-**thyon**	

Leisure/interests

Leisure

Where can I/ we go...?	**¿Dónde se puede ir a...?**
	¿**don**-de se **pwe**-de eer a...?
fishing	**pescar**
	pes**kar**
riding	**montar a caballo**
	mon**tar** a ka-**ba**-lyo
Are there any good beaches near here?	**¿Hay alguna playa buena cerca de aquí?**
	¿**a**ee al-**goo**-na **pla**-ya **bwe**-na **thair**ka de a-**kee**?
Is there a swimming pool?	**¿Hay piscina?**
	¿**a**ee pees-**thee**-na?

Music

There are often music and dance festivals in the summer. They generally begin quite late, at about 10.30 or 11 pm.

Are there any good concerts on?	**¿Dan algún buen concierto aquí?**
	¿dan al**goon** bwen kon-**thyair**-to a-**kee**?

72

Where can I get tickets?	**¿Dónde venden las entradas?**
	¿**don**de **ben**den las en-**tra**-das?
Where can we hear some flamenco/salsa?	**¿Qué sitios hay para escuchar flamenco/salsa?**
	¿ke **see**tyos **a**ee pa-ra es-koo-**char** fla-**men**-ko/**sal**sa?

Cinema

· ·

The last film showing is usually at midnight and tickets are cheaper.

v.o (versión original) bair**syon** o-ree-khee-**nal**	original version

What's on at the cinema?	**¿Qué películas ponen?**
	¿ke pe-**lee**-koo-las **po**-nen?
When does the film start?	**¿A qué hora empieza la película?**
	¿a ke **o**-ra em-**pye**-tha la pe-**lee**-koo-la?
How much are the tickets?	**¿Cuánto cuestan las entradas?**
	¿**kwan**to **kwes**tan las en-**tra**-das?

> **Making friends** (p 21)

Two for the (time) showing	**Dos para la sesión de las...**
	dos pa-ra la se-**syon** de las...

Para la sala uno/dos no quedan localidades/entradas	For screen 1/2 there are no tickets left
pa-ra la **sa**-la **oo**no/dos no **ke**-dan lo-ka-lee-**da**-des/ en-**tra**-das	

Theatre/opera

• •

Performances generally start late at about 9 or 10 pm.

el patio de butacas	stalls
el **pa**-tyo de boo-**ta**-kas	
la platea la pla-**te**-a	dress circle
el anfiteatro	upper circle
el an-fee-te-**a**-tro	
el palco el **pal**ko	box
la localidad/el asiento	seat
la lo-ka-lee-**dad**/ el a-**syen**-to	

What's on at the theatre?	**¿Qué están echando en el teatro?**
	¿ke es**tan** e-**chan**-do en el te-**a**-tro?
How do we get to the theatre?	**¿Cómo se va al teatro?**
	¿**ko**-mo se ba al te-**a**-tro?
What prices are the tickets?	**¿De qué precios son las entradas?**
	¿de ke pre-**thyos** son las en-**tra**-das?
I'd like two tickets...	**Quisiera dos entradas...**
	kee-**sye**-ra dos en-**tra**-das...
for tonight	**para esta noche**
	pa-ra **es**ta **no**-che
for tomorrow night	**para mañana por la noche**
	pa-ra ma-**nya**-na por la **no**-che
for 5th August	**para el cinco de agosto**
	pa-ra el **theen**ko de a-**go**-sto
in the stalls	**de patio de butacas**
	de **pa**-tyo de boo-**ta**-kas
in the dress circle	**de platea**
	de pla-**te**-a
in the upper circle	**de anfiteatro**
	de an-fee-te-**a**-tro
When does the performance begin/end?	**¿Cuándo empieza/termina la representación?**
	¿**kwan**do em-**pye**-tha/tair-**mee**-na la re-pre-sen-ta-**thyon**?

Television

••

Leisure

el mando (a distancia) el **man**do (a dees-**tan**-thya)	remote control
el telediario el te-le-dee-**a**-ryo	news
encender en-then-**dair**	to switch on
apagar a-pa-**gar**	to switch off
el programa el pro-**gra**-ma	programme
los dibujos animados los dee-**boo**-khos a-nee-**ma**-dos	cartoons

Where is the television?
¿Dónde está el televisor?
¿**don**de es**ta** el te-le-bee-**sor**?

How do you switch it on?
¿Cómo se enciende?
¿**ko**-mo se en-**thyen**-de?

Which button do I press?
¿Qué botón tengo que pulsar?
¿ke bo-**ton ten**go ke pool**sar**?

Please could you lower the volume?
Por favor, ¿podría bajar el volumen?
por fa-**bor**, ¿po-**dree**-a ba-**khar** el bo-**loo**-men?

May I turn the volume up?
¿Puedo subir el volumen?
¿**pwe**-do soo**beer** el bo-**loo**-men?

76

When is the news?	**¿Cúando es el telediario?**
	¿**kwan**do es el te-le-dee-**a**-ryo?
Do you have any English language channels?	**¿Hay alguna cadena en inglés?**
	¿**a**ee al-**goo**-na ka-**de**-na en een**gles**?

Sport

The easiest way to buy tickets to a football match is direct from the stadium ticket booth about an hour before kick-off. Sunday matches usually begin between 5 and 6 pm. For big Saturday night matches you would have to buy tickets in advance. Saturday night matches usually begin about 9 pm.

Where can I/ we...?	**¿Dónde se puede...?**
	¿**don**de se **pwe**-de...?
play tennis	**jugar al tenis**
	khoo**gar** al **te**-nees
play golf	**jugar al golf**
	khoo**gar** al golf
go swimming	**ir a nadar**
	eer a na-**dar**
go jogging	**hacer footing**
	a-**thair foo**teen

How much is it per hour?	**¿Cuánto cuesta la hora?**
	¿**kwan**to **kwes**ta la **o**-ra?
Do you have to be a member?	**¿Hay que ser socio?**
	¿**a**ee ke sair **so**-thyo?
Do they hire out...?	**¿Alquilan...?**
	¿al-**kee**-lan...?
rackets	**raquetas**
	ra-**ke**-tas
golf clubs	**palos de golf**
	pa-los de golf
We'd like to go to see (name of team) play	**Nos gustaría ir a ver jugar al...**
	nos goos-ta-**ree**-a eer a bair khoo**gar** al...
Where can we get tickets?	**¿Dónde venden las entradas?**
	¿**don**de **ben**den las en-**tra**-das?
How do we get to the stadium?	**¿Cómo se va al estadio?**
	¿**ko**-mo se ba al es-**ta**-dyo?

Skiing

....

el forfait el for**fey**	ski pass
el monitor/la monitora	instructor
el mo-nee-**tor**/ la mo-nee-**to**-ra	
el esquí de fondo	cross-country skiing
el es**kee** de **fon**do	

I want to hire skis	**Querría alquilar unos esquíes**
	ke-**rree**-a al-kee-**lar oo**nos es-**kee**-es
Does the price include...?	**¿El precio incluye...?**
	¿el **pre**-thyo een-**kloo**-ye...?
boots	**las botas**
	las **bo**-tas
poles	**los bastones**
	los bas-**to**-nes
Can you adjust my bindings, please?	**¿Me puede ajustar las fijaciones?**
	¿me **pwe**-de a-khoos-**tar** las fee-kha-**thyo**-nes?
How much is a pass...?	**¿Cuánto cuesta un forfait...?**
	¿**kwan**to **kwes**ta oon for**fey**...?
for a day	**para un día**
	pa-ra oon **dee**-a
per week	**semanal**
	se-ma-**nal**
When does the last chair-lift go up?	**¿Cuándo sale el último telesilla?**
	¿**kwan**do **sa**-le el **ool**-tee-mo te-le-**see**-lya?

Skiing

¿Ha esquiado alguna vez antes? ¿a es-kee-**a**-do al-**goo**-na beth **an**tes?	Have you ever skied before?
¿De qué largo quiere los esquíes? ¿de ke **lar**go **kye**-re los es-**kee**-es?	What length skis do you want?
¿Qué número de zapato usa? ¿ke **noo**-me-ro de tha-**pa**-to **oo**sa?	What is your shoe size?

Leisure

Walking

●●●●●●●●●●●●●●●●●●●●●●●●●●●●●●●●●●●●●●

Are there any guided walks?	**¿Organizan recorridos a pie con guía?**
	¿or-ga-**nee**-than re-ko-**rree**-dos a pye kon **gee**-a?
Do you have a guide to local walks?	**¿Tiene alguna guía de esta zona que traiga recorridos a pie?**
	¿**tye**-ne al-**goo**-na **gee**-a de **es**ta **tho**-na ke **traee**-ga re-ko-**rree**-dos a pye?
How many kilometres is the walk?	**¿De cuántos kilómetros es la excursión?**
	¿de **kwan**tos kee-**lo**-me-tros es la eks-koor-**syon**?
How long will it take?	**¿Cuánto se tarda?**
	¿**kwan**to se **tar**da?
Is it very steep?	**¿Hay mucha subida?**
	¿**a**ee **moo**cha soo-**bee**-da?
We'd like to go climbing	**Nos gustaría hacer montañismo**
	nos goos-ta-**ree**-a a-**thair** mon-ta-**nyees**-mo

> **Maps and guides** (p 65)

Communications

Telephone and mobile

To phone Spain from the UK, the international code is **oo 34** plus the Spanish area code (e.g. Barcelona **93**, Madrid **91**) followed by the number you require. To phone the UK from Spain, dial **oo 44** plus the UK area code without the first **o** e.g. Glasgow **(o)141**. For calls within Spain you must dial the area code and number (even for local calls).

A phonecard, please	**Una tarjeta telefónica, por favor**
	oona tar-**khe**-ta te-le-**fo**-nee-ka, por fa-**bor**
for 6/12 euros	**de seis/doce euros**
	de seys/**do**-the **eoo**-ros
I want to make a phone call	**Quiero hacer una llamada telefónica**
	kye-ro a-**thair oo**na lya-**ma**-da te-le-**fo**-nee-ka
I will give you a call	**Te daré un toque**
	te da-**re** un **to**-ke

82

Where can I buy a phonecard?	**¿Dónde venden tarjetas telefónicas?**
	¿**don**de **ben**den tar-**khe**-tas te-le-**fo**-nee-kas?
Do you have a mobile?	**¿Tiene móvil?**
	¿**tye**-ne mo-beel?
What is the number of your mobile?	**¿Cuál es su número de móvil?**
	¿kwal es soo **noo**-me-ro de **mo**-beel?
My mobile number is...	**Mi número de móvil es...**
	mee **noo**-me-ro de **mo**-beel es...
Señor Lopez, please	**El Señor López, por favor**
	el se-**nyor lo**-pez, por fa-**bor**
Extension (number)	**Extensión...**
	eks-ten-**syon**...
Can I speak to...?	**¿Puedo hablar con...?**
	¿**pwe**-do a-**blar** kon...?
I would like to speak to...	**Querría hablar con...**
	ke-**rree**-a a-**blar** kon...
Can I speak to Mr Salas?	**¿Puedo hablar con el Sr. Salas?**
	¿**pwe**-do a-**blar** kon el se-**nyor sa**-las?
Is Valle there?	**¿Está Valle?**
	¿es**ta ba**-lye?

Communications

FACE TO FACE

A **¿Diga(me)?**
¿**di**-ga(-me)?
Hello

B **Querría hablar con ..., por favor**
ke-**rree**-a a-**blar** kon ..., por fa-**bor**
I'd like to speak to ..., please

A **¿De parte de quién?**
¿de **par**te de kyen?
Who's calling?

B **Soy Daniela**
soy da-**nye**-la
It's Daniela

A **Un momento, por favor**
oon mo-**men**-to, por fa-**bor**
Just a moment, please

This is Jim Brown	**Soy Jim Brown**	
	soy jim brown	
It's me	**Soy yo**	
	soy yo	
I want to make an outside call, can I have a line?	**Querría llamar fuera, ¿me da línea?**	
	ke-**rree**-a lya-**mar fwe**-ra, ¿me da **lee**-ne-a?	
I'll call back...	**Volveré a llamar...**	
	bol-be-**re** a lya-**mar**...	
later	**más tarde**	
	mas **tar**de	

84

tomorrow	**mañana**
	ma-**nya**-na

¿Con quién hablo?/ **¿Quién es?** ¿kon kyen **a**-blo/kyen es?	Who am I talking to?
No cuelgue, por favor no **kwel**ge, por fa-**bor**	Hold the line, please
Ahora se pone a-**o**-ra se **po**-ne	He/She is coming
Está comunicando esta ko-moo-nee-**kan**-do	It's engaged
¿Puede volver a llamar más tarde? ¿**pwe**-de bol**bair** a lya-**mar** mas **tar**de?	Can you try again later?
Se ha equivocado de número se a e-kee-bo-**ka**-do de **noo**-me-ro	You have the wrong number
Deje su mensaje después de oír la señal (answering machine) **de**-khe soo men-**sa**-khe des**pwes** de o-**eer** la se-**nyal**	Please leave a message after the tone

Telephone and mobile

85

Por favor, se ruega apaguen los teléfonos móviles	Please turn your mobiles off
por fa-**bor**, se **rwe**-ga a-**pa**-gen los te-**le**-fo-nos **mo**-bee-les	

Text messaging

In mobile-phone messages accents and upside-down punctuation are often omitted.

I will text you	**Te mandaré un mensaje (al móvil)**
	te man-da-**re** oon men-**sa**-khe (al **mo**-beel)
Can you text me?	**¿Me puedes mandar un mensaje (al móvil)?**
	¿me **pwe**-des man**dar** oon men-**sa**-khe (al **mo**-beel)?
tomorrow	**mñn (mañana)**
later	**+trd (más tarde)**
goodbye	**a2 (adiós)**
where?	**dnd? (¿dónde?)**

Communications

86

let's meet	**qdms?** (¿quedamos?)
how are you?	**q tl?** (¿qué tal?)
I'll see you soon	**TBL** (te veo luego)
I love you	**t q** (te quiero)
call me	**ymam** (llámame)
why?	**xq?** (¿por qué?)
are you coming?	**vns?** (¿vienes?)
because	**xq** (porque)

E-mail

....

New message:	**Nuevo mensaje:**
To:	**Para:**
From:	**De:**
Subject:	**Asunto:**
Forward:	**Reenviar:**
Inbox:	**Bandeja de entrada:**
Sent items:	**Enviados:**
Attachment:	**Archivo adjunto:**
Send:	**Enviar:**

Do you have an e-mail?	**¿Tiene (dirección de) email?** ¿**tye**-ne (dee-rek-**thyon** de) ee-**meyl**?

What is your e-mail address?	**¿Cuál es su (dirección de) email?**
	¿kwal es soo (dee-rek-**thyon** de) ee-**meyl**?
How do you spell it?	**¿Cómo se escribe?**
	¿**ko**-mo se es-**kree**-be?
All one word	**Todo junto**
	to-do **khoon**to
All lower case	**Todo en minúscula(s)**
	to-do en mee-**noos**-koo-la(s)
My e-mail address is...	**Mi (dirección de) email es...**
	mee (dee-rek-**thyon** de) ee-**meyl** es...
caroline.smith@ bit.co.uk	**caroline punto smith arroba bit punto co punto uk**
	caroline **poon**to smith a-**rro**-ba bit **poon**to ko **poon**to oo ka
Can I send an e-mail?	**¿Puedo mandar un email?**
	¿**pwe**-do man-**dar** oon ee-**meyl**?
Did you get my e-mail?	**¿Le llegó mi email?**
	¿le lye-**go** mee ee-**meyl**?

Internet

•••••••••••••••••••••••••••••••••••

Are there any internet cafés here?	**¿Hay algún cibercafé aquí?** ¿**a**ee al**goon** thee-bair-ka-**fe** a-**kee**?
How much is it to log on for an hour?	**¿Cuánto cuesta una hora de conexión?** ¿**kwan**to **kwes**ta **oo**na **o**-ra de ko-nek-**syon**?
The website address is...	**La página (web) es...** la **pa**-khee-na (web) es...
www.collins.co.uk	**www.collins.co.uk** **oo**be **do**-ble **oo**be **do**-ble **oo**be **do**-ble **poon**to collins **poon**to ko **poon**to oo ka
I can't log on	**No puedo conectarme** no **pwe**-do ko-nek-**tar**-me

Fax

● ●

To fax Spain from the UK, the code is **oo 34**
followed by the Spanish area code, e.g. Madrid **91**,
Bilbao 94, and the fax number.

Addressing a fax

de	from
a la atención de	for the attention of
fecha	date
con referencia a	re:
este documento	this document
contiene...	contains...
páginas, ésta inclusive	pages including this one

Do you have a fax?	**¿Tiene fax?**
	¿**tye**-ne faks?
I want to send	**Querría mandar un fax**
a fax	ke-**rree**-a man**dar** oon faks
Please resend	**Por favor, vuélvame a**
your fax	**mandar su fax**
	por fa-**bor**, **bwel**-ba-me a
	man**dar** soo faks
I can't read it	**No se entiende**
	no se en-**tyen**-de

Practicalities

Money

Banks are generally open 8.30 am to 2 pm Monday to Friday, with some banks open on Saturday mornings. Double-check opening hours when you arrive as these change during the summer. The Spanish currency is the **euro** (**eoo**-ro). Euro cents are known as **céntimos** (**then**-tee-mos).

la tarjeta de crédito la tar-**khe**-ta de **kre**-dee-to	credit card
pagar en efectivo pa-**gar** en e-fek-**tee**-bo	pay in cash
la factura la fak-**too**-ra	invoice
los cheques de viaje los **che**-kes de **bya**-khe	traveller's cheques

Where can I/we change some money?
¿Dónde se puede cambiar dinero?
¿**don**de se **pwe**-de kam-**byar** dee-**ne**-ro?

I want to change these traveller's cheques	**Quiero cambiar estos cheques de viaje** **kye**-ro kam**byar es**tos **che**-kes de **bya**-khe
When does the bank open/close?	**¿Cuándo abren/cierran el banco?** ¿**kwan**do **a**-bren/**thye**-rran el **ban**ko?
Can I pay with pounds/euros?	**¿Puedo pagar con libras/euros?** ¿**pwe**-do pa-**gar** kon **lee**bras/**eoo**-ros?
Where is the nearest cash dispenser?	**¿Dónde está el cajero más cercano?** ¿**don**de es**ta** el ka-**khe**-ro mas thair-**ka**-no?
Can I use my card with this cash dispenser?	**¿Puedo usar mi tarjeta en este cajero?** ¿**pwe**-do oo**sar** mee tar-**khe**-ta en **es**te ka-**khe**-ro?
Do you have any small change?	**¿Tiene suelto?** ¿**tye**-ne **swel**to?

Paying

....

el importe el eem-**por**-te	amount to be paid
la cuenta la **kwen**ta	bill
la factura la fak-**too**-ra	invoice
abone el importe en caja a-**bo**-ne el eem-**por**-te en **ka**-kha	pay at the cash desk
el tique (de compra) el **tee**ke de **kom**pra	till receipt

How much is it?	**¿Cuánto es?** ¿**kwan**to es?
How much will it be?	**¿Cuánto me costará?** ¿**kwan**to me kos-ta-**ra**?
Can I pay...?	**¿Puedo pagar...?** ¿**pwe**-do pa-**gar**...?
by credit card	**con tarjeta de crédito** kon tar-**khe**-ta de **kre**-dee-to
by cheque	**con talón/(un) cheque** kon ta-**lon**/(oon) **che**-ke
Do you take credit cards?	**¿Aceptan tarjetas de crédito?** ¿a-**thep**-tan tar-**khe**-tas de **kre**-dee-to?
Is VAT included?	**¿Está incluido el IVA?** ¿Es**ta** een-kloo-**ee**-do el **ee**ba?
Put it on my bill	**Póngalo en mi cuenta** **pon**-ga-lo en mee **kwen**ta

I need a receipt, please	**Necesito un recibo, por favor** ne-the-**see**-to oon re-**thee**-bo, por fa-**bor**
Where do I pay?	**¿Dónde se paga?** ¿**Don**de se **pa**-ga?
I'm sorry	**Lo siento** lo **syen**to
I've nothing smaller	**No tengo cambio** no **ten**go **kam**byo

Luggage

consigna kon-**seeg**-na	left luggage office
consignas automáticas kon-**seeg**-nas ow-to-**ma**-tee-kas	luggage lockers
el carrito el ka-**rree**-to	luggage trolley

My luggage hasn't arrived	**Mi equipaje no ha llegado** mee e-kee-**pa**-khe no a lye-**ga**-do
My suitcase has arrived damaged	**La maleta ha llegado estropeada** la ma-**le**-ta a lye-**ga**-do es-tro-pe-**a**-da
What's happened to the luggage on the flight from...?	**¿Qué ha pasado con el equipaje del vuelo de...?** ¿ke a pa-**sa**-do kon el e-kee-**pa**-khe del **bwe**-lo de...?

> **Train** (p 32) > **Air travel** (p 38)

Practicalities

Repairs

• •

Repairs while you wait are known as **reparaciones en el acto**.

This is broken	**Se me ha roto esto**
	se me a **ro**-to **es**to
Where can I get this repaired?	**¿Dónde me lo pueden arreglar?**
	¿**don**de me lo **pwe**-den a-**rre**-glar?
Is it worth repairing?	**¿Merece la pena arreglarlo?**
	¿me-**re**-the la **pe**-na a-rre-**glar**-lo?
Can you repair...?	**¿Puede arreglarme...?**
	¿**pwe**-de a-rre-**glar**-me...?
these shoes	**estos zapatos**
	estos tha-**pa**-tos
my watch	**el reloj**
	el re-**lokh**
How much will it be?	**¿Cuánto me costará?**
	¿**kwan**to me kos-ta-**ra**?
Can you do it straightaway?	**¿Me lo puede hacer en el acto?**
	¿me lo **pwe**-de a-**thair** en el **ak**to?
How long will it take to repair?	**¿Cuánto tardarán en arreglarlo?**
	¿**kwan**to tar-da-**ran** en a-rre-**glar**-lo?

> **Breakdown** (p 45)

| When will it be ready? | ¿Para cuándo estará? |
| | ¿pa-ra **kwan**do es-ta-**ra**? |

Laundry

· ·

la tintorería	dry-cleaner's
la teen-to-re-**ree**-a	
la lavandería automática	launderette
la la-ban-de-**ree**-a	
ow-to-**ma**-tee-ka	
el detergente en polvo	washing powder
el de-tair-**khen**-te en **pol**vo	

Where can I do some washing?	¿Dónde puedo lavar algo de ropa?
	¿**don**de **pwe**-do la-**bar al**go de **ro**-pa?
Is there a launderette near here?	¿Hay alguna lavandería automática por aquí cerca?
	¿**aee** al-**goo**-na la-ban-de-**ree**-a ow-to-**ma**-tee-ka por a-**kee thair**ka?
Is there somewhere to dry clothes?	¿Hay algún sitio para secar la ropa?
	¿**aee** al**goon see**tyo pa-ra se-**kar** la **ro**-pa?

Complaints

....

This doesn't work	**Esto no funciona**
	esto no foon-**thyo**-na
The ... doesn't work	**El/La ... no funciona**
	el/la ... no foon-**thyo**-na
The ... don't work	**Los/Las ... no funcionan**
	los/las ... no foon-**thyo**-nan
light	**la luz**
	la looth
heating	**la calefacción**
	la ka-le-fak-**thyon**
air conditioning	**el aire acondicionado**
	el **aee**-re a-kon-dee-thyo-**na**-do
There's a problem with the room	**Hay un problema con la habitación**
	aee oon pro-**ble**-ma kon la a-bee-ta-**thyon**
It's noisy	**Hay mucho ruido**
	aee **moo**cho **rwee**do
It's too hot (room)	**Hace demasiado calor**
	a-the de-ma-**sya**-do ka-**lor**
It's too cold (room)	**Hace demasiado frío**
	a-the de-ma-**sya**-do **free**-o
It's too hot/too cold (food)	**Está muy caliente/muy frío**
	es**ta** mwee ka-**lyen**-te/mwee **free**-o

The meat is cold	**La carne está fría**
	la **kar**ne es**ta free**-a
This isn't what I ordered	**Esto no es lo que yo he pedido**
	esto no es lo ke yo e pe-**dee**-do
It's faulty	**Tiene un defecto**
	tye-ne oon de-**fek**-to
It's dirty	**Está sucio**
	es**ta soo**thyo
I want my money back	**Quiero que me devuelvan el dinero**
	kye-ro ke me de-**bwel**-ban el dee-**ne**-ro

Problems

• •

Can you help me?	**¿Me puede ayudar?**
	¿me **pwe**-de a-yoo-**dar**?
I only speak a little Spanish	**Sólo hablo un poco de español**
	so-lo **a**-blo oon **po**-ko de es-pa-**nyol**
Does anyone here speak English?	**¿Hay aquí alguien que hable inglés?**
	¿**a**ee a-**kee al**gyen ke **a**-ble een**gles**?
What's the matter?	**¿Qué pasa?**
	¿ke **pa**-sa?

I'm lost	**Me he perdido**
	me e pair-**dee**-do
How do I get to...?	**¿Cómo voy a...?**
	¿**ko**-mo boy a...?
I've missed...	**He perdido...**
	e pair-**dee**-do...
my train	**el tren**
	el tren
my plane	**el avión**
	el a-**byon**
my connection	**el enlace**
	el en-**la**-the
I've missed my flight because there was a strike	**He perdido el vuelo porque había una huelga**
	e pair-**dee**-do el **bwe**-lo **por**ke a-**bee**-a **oo**na **wel**ga
The coach has left without me	**Se ha ido el autocar y me ha dejado aquí**
	se a **ee**do el ow-to-**kar** ee me a de-**kha**-do a-**kee**
Can you show me how this works?	**¿Me puede enseñar como funciona esto?**
	¿me **pwe**-de en-se-**nyar ko**-mo foon-**thyo**-na **es**to?
I have lost my purse	**He perdido el monedero**
	e pair-**dee**-do el mo-ne-**de**-ro
I need to get to...	**Tengo que ir a...**
	tengo ke eer a...

Leave me alone!	¡Déjeme en paz!
	¡**de**-khe-me en path!
Go away!	¡Váyase!
	¡**ba**-ya-se!

Emergencies

. . . .

The emergency number for the police is **091**. If you need an ambulance, they will arrange it.

la policía la po-lee-**thee**-a	police
la ambulancia la am-boo-**lan**-thya	ambulance
los bomberos los bom-**be**-ros	fire brigade
urgencias oor-**khen**-thyas	casualty department

Help!	¡Socorro!
	¡so-**ko**-rro!
Fire!	¡Fuego!
	¡**fwe**-go!
There's been an accident	Ha habido un accidente
	a a-**bee**-do oon ak-thee-**den**-te
Someone is injured	Hay un herido
	aee oon e-**ree**-do

Someone has been knocked down by a car	**Han atropellado a alguien** an a-tro-pe-**lya**-do a **al**gyen
Call...	**Llame a...** **lya**-me a...
the police	**la policía** la po-lee-**thee**-a
an ambulance	**una ambulancia** **oo**na am-boo-**lan**-thya
please	**por favor** por fa-**bor**
Where is the police station?	**¿Dónde está la comisaría?** ¿**don**de es**ta** la ko-mee-sa-**ree**-a?
I want to report a theft	**Quiero denunciar un robo** **kye**-ro de-noon-**thyar** oon **ro**-bo
I've been robbed/ attacked	**Me han robado/agredido** me an ro-**ba**-do/a-gre-**dee**-do
Someone's stolen my...	**Me han robado...** me an ro-**ba**-do...
bag	**el bolso** el **bol**so
traveller's cheques	**los cheques de viaje** los **che**-kes de **bya**-khe
My car has been broken into	**Me han entrado en el coche** me an en-**tra**-do en el **ko**-che
My car has been stolen	**Me han robado el coche** me an ro-**ba**-do el **ko**-che
I've been raped	**Me han violado** me an byo-**la**-do

I want to speak to a policewoman	**Quiero hablar con una mujer policía**
	kye-ro a-**blar** kon **oo**na moo**khair** po-lee-**thee**-a
I need to make an urgent telephone call	**Necesito hacer una llamada urgente**
	ne-the-**see**-to a-**thair** **oo**na lya-**ma**-da oor-**khen**-te
I need a report for my insurance	**Necesito un informe para el seguro**
	ne-the-**see**-to oon een-**for**-me pa-ra el se-**goo**-ro
How much is the fine?	**¿De cuánto es la multa?**
	¿de **kwan**to es la **mool**ta?
Where do I pay it?	**¿Dónde la pago?**
	¿**don**de la **pa**-go?
Do I have to pay it straightaway?	**¿Tengo que pagarla inmediatamente?**
	¿**ten**go ke pa-**gar**-la een-me-dya-ta-**men**-te?
I'm very sorry	**Lo siento mucho**
	lo **syen**to moo**cho**

Practicalities

YOU MAY HEAR...

Se ha saltado el semáforo en rojo se a sal-**ta**-do el se-**ma**-fo-ro en **ro**-kho	You went through a red light

Health

Pharmacy

• •

la farmacia la far-**ma**-thya	pharmacy/chemist
la farmacia de guardia la far-**ma**-thya de **gwar**dya	duty chemist
la receta médica la re-**the**-ta **me**-dee-ka	prescription

Have you   **¿Tiene algo para...?**
   something for...?   ¿**tye**-ne **al**go pa-ra...?
a headache   **el dolor de cabeza**
   el do-**lor** de ka-**be**-tha
car sickness   **el mareo**
   el ma-**re**-o
diarrhoea   **la diarrea**
   la dee-a-**rre**-a
I have a rash   **Me ha salido un sarpullido**
   me a sa-**lee**-do oon
     sar-poo-**lyee**-do
I feel sick   **Tengo naúseas**
   tengo **now**-se-as

103

Is it safe for children?	¿Lo pueden tomar los niños?
	¿lo **pwe**-den to-**mar** los **nee**nyos?
How much should I give?	¿Cuánto le doy?
	¿**kwan**to le doy?

YOU MAY HEAR...

| Tómelo tres veces al día antes de/con/después de las comidas | Take it three times a day before/with/ after meals |
| **to**-me-lo tres **be**-thes al **dee**-a **an**tes de/kon/ des**pwes** de las ko-**mee**-das | |

Body

. . . .

In Spanish the possessive (my, his, her, etc.) is generally not used with parts of the body, e.g.

| <u>My</u> head hurts | Me duele <u>la</u> cabeza |
| <u>My</u> hands are dirty | Tengo <u>las</u> manos sucias |

ankle	el tobillo	to-**bee**-lyo
arm	el brazo	**bra**-tho
back	la espalda	es-**pal**-da

bone	el hueso	**we**-so
ear	la oreja/el oído	o-**re**-kha/o-**ee**-do
eye	el ojo	**o**-kho
finger	el dedo	**de**-do
foot	el pie	pye
hand	la mano	**ma**-no
head	la cabeza	ka-**be**-tha
heart	el corazón	ko-ra-**thon**
hip	la cadera	ka-**de**-ra
kidney	el riñón	reen**yon**
knee	la rodilla	ro-**dee**-lya
leg	la pierna	**pyair**na
liver	el hígado	**ee**-ga-do
mouth	la boca	**bo**-ka
nail	la uña	**oo**nya
neck	el cuello	**kwe**-lyo
nose	la nariz	na-**reeth**
stomach	el estómago	es-**to**-ma-go
throat	la garganta	gar-**gan**-ta
toe	el dedo del pie	**de**-do del pye
wrist	la muñeca	moo-**nye**-ka

Body

Doctor

If you need to see a doctor, simply visit the nearest clinic with your E111 card and ask for an appointment. You usually need to go in the morning (9 am) to get a ticket for an appointment later in the day.

FACE TO FACE

A ¿Qué le pasa/ocurre?
¿ke le **pa**-sa/o-**koo**-rre?
What's wrong?

B Me encuentro mal/No me encuentro bien
me en-**kwen**-tro mal/no me en-**kwen**-tro byen
I feel ill

A ¿Tiene fiebre?
¿**tye**-ne **fye**-bre?
Do you have a temperature?

B No, me duele aquí
no, me **dwe**-le a-**kee**
No, I have a pain here *(point)*

I need a doctor	**Necesito un médico** ne-the-**see**-to oon **me**-dee-ko
My son/daughter is ill	**Mi hijo/hija está enfermo(a)** mee **ee**kho/**ee**kha es**ta** en-**fair**-mo(a)
He/She has a temperature	**Tiene fiebre** **tye**-ne **fye**-bre

I'm diabetic	**Soy diabético(a)**
	soy dya-**be**-tee-ko(a)
I'm pregnant	**Estoy embarazada**
	es**toy** em-ba-ra-**tha**-da
I'm on the pill	**Tomo la píldora**
	to-mo la **peel**-do-ra
I'm allergic to penicillin	**Soy alérgico(a) a la penicilina**
	soy a-**lair**-khee-ko(a) a la pe-nee-thee-**lee**-na
My blood group is...	**Mi grupo sanguíneo es...**
	mee **groo**po san-**gee**-ne-o es...
Will he/she have to go to hospital?	**¿Tendrá que ir al hospital?** ¿ten**dra** ke eer al os-pee-**tal**?
Will I have to pay?	**¿Tengo que pagar?**
	¿**ten**go ke pa-**gar**?
How much will it cost?	**¿Cuánto va a costar?**
	¿**kwan**to ba a kost**ar**?
I need a receipt for the insurance	**Necesito un recibo para el seguro**
	ne-the-**see**-to oon re-**thee**-bo pa-ra el se-**goo**-ro

YOU MAY HEAR...

Tiene que ingresar **tye**-ne ke een-gre-**sar**	You will have to be admitted to hospital
No es grave no es **gra**-ve	It's not serious

Doctor

> **Emergencies** (p 100)

Dentist

All dental provision is private. Simply book an appointment. It is advisable to get a quote in advance for any work to be done.

el empaste	el em-**pas**-te	filling
la funda	la **foon**da	crown
la dentadura postiza		dentures
la den-ta-**doo**-ra		
pos-**tee**-tha		

I need a dentist	**Necesito un dentista**
	ne-the-**see**-to oon den-**tees**-ta
He/She has toothache	**Tiene dolor de muelas**
	tye-ne do-**lor** de **mwe**-las
Can you do a temporary filling?	**¿Puede hacer un empaste provisional?**
	¿**pwe**-de a-**thair** oon em-**pas**-te pro-bee-syo-**nal**?
It hurts (me)	**Me duele**
	me **dwe**-le
Can you give me something for the pain?	**¿Puede darme algo para el dolor?**
	¿**pwe**-de **dar**me **al**go pa-ra el do-**lor**?

Can you repair my dentures?	¿Puede arreglarme la dentadura postiza?
	¿**pwe**-de a-rre-**glar**-me la den-ta-**doo**-ra pos-**tee**-tha?
Do I have to pay?	¿Tengo que pagar?
	¿**ten**go ke pa-**gar**?
How much will it be?	¿Cuánto me va a costar?
	¿**kwan**to me ba a kos**tar**?

YOU MAY HEAR...

Hay que sacarla	It has to come out
aee ke sa-**kar**-la	
Voy a ponerle una inyección	I'm going to give you an injection
boy a po-**nair**-le **oo**na een-yek-**thyon**	

Dentist

109

Different types of travellers

Disabled travellers

What facilities do you have for disabled people?	**¿Qué instalaciones tienen para minusválidos?** ¿ke eens-ta-la-**thyo**-nes **tye**-nen pa-ra mee-noos-**ba**-lee-dos?
Are there any toilets for the disabled?	**¿Hay aseos para minusválidos?** ¿**a**ee a-**se**-os pa-ra mee-noos-**ba**-lee-dos?
Do you have any bedrooms on the ground floor?	**¿Tienen alguna habitación en la planta baja?** ¿**tye**-nen al-**goo**-na a-bee-ta-**thyon** en la **plan**ta **ba**-kha?
Is there a lift?	**¿Hay ascensor?** ¿**a**ee as-then-**sor**?
Where is the lift?	**¿Dónde está el ascensor?** ¿**don**de es**ta** el as-then-**sor**?
Is there an induction loop?	**¿Hay audífonos?** ¿**a**ee ow-**dee**-fo-nos?
Do you have wheelchairs?	**¿Tienen sillas de ruedas?** ¿**tye**-nen **see**lyas de **rwe**-das?

 > **Hotel (booking)** (p 50)

Can you visit ... in a wheelchair?	¿Se puede visitar ... en silla de ruedas?
	¿se **pwe**-de bee-see-**tar** ... en **see**lya de **rwe**-das?
Is there a reduction for disabled people?	¿Hacen descuento a los minusválidos?
	¿**a**-then des-**kwen**-to a los mee-noos-**ba**-lee-dos?
Is there somewhere I can sit down?	¿Hay algún sitio donde pueda sentarme?
	¿**a**ee al**goon see**tyo **don**de **pwe**-da sen-**tar**-me?

With kids

. . . .

Public transport is free for children under 4. Children between 4 and 12 pay half price.

A child's ticket	Un billete de niño
	oon bee-**lye**-te de **neen**yo
He/She is ... years old	Tiene ... años
	tye-ne ... **a**-nyos
Is there a reduction for children?	¿Hay descuento para niños?
	¿**a**ee des-**kwen**-to pa-ra **neen**yos?
Do you have a children's menu?	¿Tiene menú para niños?
	¿**tye**-ne me-**noo** pa-ra **neen**yos?

111

Is it OK to take children?	¿Está permitido llevar niños?
	¿es**ta** pair-mee-**tee**-do **lye**-bar **nee**nyos?
What is there for children to do?	¿Qué cosas hay para los niños?
	¿ke **ko**-sas **a**ee pa-ra los **nee**nyos?
Is there a play park near here?	¿Hay algún parque infantil por aquí cerca?
	¿**a**ee al**goon par**ke een-fan-**teel** por a-**kee thair**ka?
Is it safe for children?	¿Es seguro para los niños?
	¿es se-**goo**-ro pa-ra los **nee**nyos?
Do you have...?	¿Tiene...?
	¿**tye**-ne...?
a high chair	una trona
	oona **tro**-na
a cot	una cuna
	oona **koo**na
I have two children	Tengo dos hijos
	tengo dos **ee**khos
He/She is 10 years old	Tiene diez años
	tye-ne dyeth **a**-nyos

> **Doctor** (p 106)

Reference

Alphabet

The Spanish alphabet treats **ch**, **ll** and **ñ** as separate letters. Below are the words used for clarification when spelling something out.

¿Cómo se escribe?	How do you spell it?
¿**ko**-mo se es-**kree**-be?	
A de Antonio, B de Barcelona	A for Antonio, B for Barcelona
a de an-**to**-nyo, be de bar-the-**lo**-na	

A	a	**Antonio**	an-**to**-nyo
B	be	**Barcelona**	bar-the-**lo**-na
C	the	**Carmen**	**kar**men
CH	che	**Chocolate**	cho-ko-**la**-te
D	de	**Dolores**	do-**lo**-res
E	e	**Enrique**	en-**rree**-ke
F	**e**-fe	**Francia**	**fran**thya
G	khe	**Gerona**	khe-**ro**-na

H	**a**-che	**Historia**	ees-**to**-rya
I	ee	**Inés**	ee**nes**
J	**kho**-ta	**José**	kho-**se**
K	ka	**Kilo**	**kee**lo
L	**e**-le	**Lorenzo**	lo-**ren**-tho
LL	**e**-lye	**Lluvia**	**lyoo**bya
M	**e**-me	**Madrid**	ma-**dreed**
N	**e**-ne	**Navarra**	na-**ba**-rra
Ñ	**e**-nye	**Ñoño**	**nyo**-nyo
O	o	**Oviedo**	o-**bye**-do
P	pe	**París**	pa-**rees**
Q	koo	**Querido**	ke-**ree**-do
R	**e**-re	**Carta**	**kar**ta
RR	**e**-rre	**Carrete**	ka-**rre**-te
S	**e**-se	**Sábado**	**sa**-ba-do
T	te	**Tarragona**	ta-rra-**go**-na
U	oo	**Ulises**	oo-**lee**-ses
V	**oo**be	**Valencia**	ba-**len**-thya
W	**oo**be **do**-ble	**Washington**	**wa**-seen-ton
X	**e**-kees	**Xilófono**	see-**lo**-fo-no
Y	ee **grye**-ga	**Yegua**	**ye**-gwa
Z	**the**-ta	**Zaragoza**	tha-ra-**go**-tha

Measurements and quantities

••

1 lb = approx. 0.5 kilo – 1 pint = approx. 0.5 litre

Liquids

1/2 litre of...	**medio litro de...**
	me-dyo **lee**tro de...
a litre of...	**un litro de...**
	oon **lee**tro de...
1/2 bottle of...	**media botella de...**
	me-dya bo-**te**-lya de...
a bottle of...	**una botella de...**
	oona bo-**te**-lya de...
a glass of...	**un vaso de...**
	oon **ba**-so de...

Weights

100 grams of...	**cien gramos de...**
	thyen **gra**-mos de...
1/2 kilo of...	**medio kilo de...**
	me-dyo **kee**lo de...
a kilo of...	**un kilo de...**
	oon **kee**lo de...

Food

a slice of...	**una loncha de...**
	oona **lon**cha de...
a portion of...	**una ración de...**
	oona ra-**thyon** de...
a dozen...	**una docena de...**
	oona do-**the**-na de...
a box of...	**una caja de...**
	oona **ka**-kha de...
a packet of...	**un paquete de...**
	oon pa-**ke**-te de...
a tin of...	**una lata de...**
	oona **la**-ta de...
a jar of...	**un tarro de...**
	oon **ta**-rro de...

Miscellaneous

10 euros worth of...	**diez euros de...**	
	dyeth **eoo**-ros de...	
a quarter	**un cuarto**	oon **kwar**to
ten per cent	**el diez por ciento**	
	el dyeth por **thyen**to	
more...	**más...**	mas...
less...	**menos...**	**me**-nos...
enough	**bastante**	bas-**tan**-te
double	**el doble**	el **do**-ble
twice	**dos veces**	dos **be**-thes

Numbers

• •

0	**cero the**-ro
1	**uno oo**no
2	**dos** dos
3	**tres** tres
4	**cuatro kwa**-tro
5	**cinco theen**ko
6	**seis** seys
7	**siete sye**-te
8	**ocho o**-cho
9	**nueve nwe**-be
10	**diez** dyeth
11	**once on**the
12	**doce do**-the
13	**trece tre**-the
14	**catorce** ka-**tor**-the
15	**quince keen**the
16	**dieciséis** dye-thee-**seys**
17	**diecisiete** dye-thee-**sye**-te
18	**dieciocho** dye-thee-**o**-cho
19	**diecinueve** dye-thee-**nwe**-be
20	**veinte beyn**te
21	**veintiuno** beyn-tee-**oo**-no
22	**veintidós** beyn-tee-**dos**
23	**veintitrés** beyn-tee-**tres**
24	**veinticuatro** beyn-tee-**kwa**-tro

30	**treinta** treynta	
40	**cuarenta** kwa-**ren**-ta	
50	**cincuenta** theen-**kwen**-ta	
60	**sesenta** se-**sen**-ta	
70	**setenta** se-**ten**-ta	
80	**ochenta** o-**chen**-ta	
90	**noventa** no-**ben**-ta	
100	**cien** thyen	
110	**ciento diez thyen**to dyeth	
500	**quinientos** kee-**nyen**-tos	
1,000	**mil** meel	
2,000	**dos mil** dos meel	
1 million	**un millón** oon mee**lyon**	

1st	**primer(o) 1ᵉʳ/1º** pree-**me**-ro		6th	**sexto 6º** **seks**to
2nd	**segundo 2º** se-**goon**-do		7th	**séptimo 7º** **sep**-tee-mo
3rd	**tercer(o) 3ᵉʳ/3º** tair-**the**-ro		8th	**octavo 8º** ok-**ta**-bo
4th	**cuarto 4º** **kwar**to		9th	**noveno 9º** no-**be**-no
5th	**quinto 5º** **keen**to		10th	**décimo 10º** **de**-thee-mo

Days and months

Days

Monday	**lunes**	**loo**nes
Tuesday	**martes**	**mar**tes
Wednesday	**miércoles**	**myair**-ko-les
Thursday	**jueves**	**khwe**-bes
Friday	**viernes**	**byair**nes
Saturday	**sábado**	**sa**-ba-do
Sunday	**domingo**	do-**meen**-go

Months

January	**enero**	e-**ne**-ro
February	**febrero**	fe-**bre**-ro
March	**marzo**	**mar**tho
April	**abril**	a-**breel**
May	**mayo**	**ma**-yo
June	**junio**	**khoo**nyo
July	**julio**	**khool**yo
August	**agosto**	a-**gos**-to
September	**septiembre**	sep-**tyem**-bre
October	**octubre**	ok-**too**-bre
November	**noviembre**	no-**byem**-bre
December	**diciembre**	dee-**thyem**-bre

Seasons

spring	**la primavera**	la pree-ma-**be**-ra
summer	**el verano**	el be-**ra**-no
autumn	**el otoño**	el o-**to**-nyo
winter	**el invierno**	el een-**byair**-no

What is today's date?	**¿Qué fecha es hoy?**
	¿ke **fe**-cha es oy?
What day is it today?	**¿Qué día es hoy?**
	¿ke **dee**-a es oy?
It's the 5th of July 2006	**Es cinco de julio de dos mil seis**
	es **theen**ko de **khoo**lyo de dos meel seys
on Saturday	**el sábado**
	el **sa**-ba-do
on Saturdays	**los sábados**
	los **sa**-ba-dos
every Saturday	**todos los sábados**
	to-dos los **sa**-ba-dos
this Saturday	**este sábado**
	este **sa**-ba-do
next Saturday	**el sábado que viene**
	el **sa**-ba-do ke **bye**-ne
last Saturday	**el sábado pasado**
	el **sa**-ba-do pa-**sa**-do
in June	**en junio**
	en **khoo**nyo

at the beginning of June	**a primeros de junio**
	a pree-**me**-ros de **khoo**nyo
at the end of June	**a finales de junio**
	a fee-**na**-les de **khoo**nyo
before summer	**antes del verano**
	antes del be-**ra**-no
during the summer	**en el verano**
	en el be-**ra**-no
after summer	**después del verano**
	des**pwes** del be-**ra**-no

Time

. . . .

The 24-hour clock is used a lot more in Europe than in Britain. After 1200 midday, it continues: **1300 - las trece**, **1400 - las catorce**, **1500 - las quince**, etc. until **2400 - las veinticuatro**. With the 24-hour clock, the words **cuarto** (quarter) and **media** (half) aren't used:

13:15 (1.15 pm)	**las trece quince/**
	(la una y cuarto)
19:30 (7.30 pm)	**las diecinueve treinta/**
	(las siete y media)
22:45 (10.45 pm)	**las veintidós cuarenta y cinco/**
	(las once menos cuarto)

What time is it, please?	**¿Qué hora es, por favor?**
	¿ke **o**-ra es, por fa-**bor**?
am	**de la mañana**
	de la ma-**nya**-na
pm	**de la tarde**
	de la **tar**de
It's...	**Son...**
	son...
2 o'clock	**las dos**
	las dos
3 o'clock	**las tres**
	las tres
6 o'clock (etc.)	**las seis**
	las seys
It's 1 o'clock	**Es la una**
	es la **oo**na
It's 1200 midday	**Son las doce del mediodía**
	son las **do**-the del me-dyo-**dee**-a
At midnight	**A medianoche**
	a me-dya-**no**-che
9	**las nueve**
	las **nwe**-be
9.10	**las nueve y diez**
	las **nwe**-be ee dyeth
quarter past 9	**las nueve y cuarto**
	las **nwe**-be ee **kwar**to
9.20	**las nueve y veinte**
	las **nwe**-be ee **beyn**te

Reference

122

9.30	**las nueve y media**
	las **nwe**-be ee **me**-dya
9.35	**las diez menos veinticinco**
	las dyeth **me**-nos
	beyn-tee-**theen**-ko
quarter to 10	**las diez menos cuarto**
	las dyeth **me**-nos **kwar**to
10 to 10	**las diez menos diez**
	las dyeth **me**-nos dyeth

Time phrases

. . . .

When does it open/close?	**¿Cuándo abre/cierra?**
	¿**kwan**do **a**-bre/**thye**-rra?
When does it begin/finish?	**¿Cuándo empieza/termina?**
	¿**kwan**do em-**pye**-tha/
	tair-**mee**-na?
at 3 o'clock	**a las tres**
	a las tres
before 3 o'clock	**antes de las tres**
	antes de las tres
after 3 o'clock	**después de las tres**
	des**pwes** de las tres
today	**hoy**
	oy

tonight	**esta noche**
	esta **no**-che
tomorrow	**mañana**
	ma-**nya**-na
yesterday	**ayer**
	a-**yair**
in the morning	**por la mañana**
	por la ma-**nya**-na
this morning	**esta mañana**
	esta ma-**nya**-na
in the afternoon	**por la tarde** (until dusk)
	por la **tar**de
in the evening	**por la tarde/por la noche**
	(late evening or night)
	por la **tar**de/por la **no**-che

Eating out

Eating places

Tapas A popular and inexpensive venue is the Tapas bar – you'll find these wherever you go. It is a good way of trying out different foods.

Cafetería Normally serves some hot dishes as well as toasted sandwiches (**sándwiches**) and cakes (**pasteles**).

Panadería Bakery. They often sell snacks and sweets.

Pastelería Cake shop

Confitería Cake shop

Bodega A wine cellar. Rather like a wine bar which serves food.

Restaurante Mealtimes are late in Spain. Lunch is generally served from 1 to 4.30 pm and dinner from 8 to 11.30 pm. The menu is usually displayed outside.

Chiringuito Beach bar/café

Mesón Traditional-style tavern restaurant.

Heladería Ice-cream parlour which also serves milkshakes: **batidos**.

In a bar/café

If you want a strong black coffee ask for **un café solo**. For a white coffee ask for **un café con leche**. Tea in Spain tends to be served weak and with lemon. And be careful not to ask for tea with milk, as it is likely that the tea bag would be put straight into hot milk. It is best to ask for the milk served separately (**aparte**).

¿Qué desea?/¿Qué va a tomar?
¿ke de-**se**-a?/¿ke ba a to-**mar**?
What will you have?

Un café con leche, por favor
oon ka-**fe** kon **le**-che, por fa-**bor**
A white coffee, please

a coffee	**un café**
	oon ka-**fe**
a lager	**una cerveza**
	oona thair-**be**-tha
a dry sherry	**un fino**
	oon **fee**no
...please	**...por favor**
	...por fa-**bor**
a tea...	**un té...**
	oon te...
with the milk	**con la leche aparte**
apart	kon la **le**-che a-**par**-te
with lemon	**con limón**
	kon lee**mon**
for two	**para dos**
	pa-ra dos
for me	**para mí**
	pa-ra mee

for him/her	**para él/ella**
	pa-ra el/**e**-lya
for us	**para nosotros**
	pa-ra no-**so**-tros
with ice, please	**con hielo, por favor**
	kon **ye**-lo, por fa-**bor**
no sugar	**sin azúcar**
	seen a-**thoo**-kar
Have you sweetener?	**¿Tiene sacarina?**
	¿**tye**-ne sa-ka-**ree**-na?
A bottle of mineral water	**Una botella de agua mineral**
	oona bo-**te**-lya de **a**-gwa mee-ne-**ral**
sparkling	**con gas**
	kon gas
still	**sin gas**
	sin gas

Other drinks to try

un café con hielo iced coffee
un chocolate rich-tasting hot chocolate, often served with **churros**
una horchata refreshing tiger nut (chufa nut) milk
un zumo juice: **de melocotón** peach, **de tomate** tomato
un anís aniseed apéritif
un batido milkshake: **de chocolate** chocolate, **de fresa** strawberry, **de vainilla** vanilla

Reading the menu

Restaurants will usually have the menu displayed next to the entrance. If you don't want a full meal, **tapas** are an ideal way of trying out the different tastes of Spain. A list of **tapas** can be found on page 137.

platos combinados usually meat or fish served with rice, chips or potatoes and vegetables

menú del día 3-course meal often including wine

desayunos y meriendas breakfasts and snacks

tapas y raciones tapas and portions. Portions are a larger helping of tapas

la carta	menu
entremeses	starters
sopas	soups
ensalada	salads
carnes	meat
pescados	fish
huevos	egg dishes
revueltos	scrambled egg cooked with mushroom, spinach or asparagus

pastas	pasta
arroz	rice dishes
quesos	cheese
postres	desserts
bebidas	drinks

In a restaurant

If you are vegetarian, or prefer vegetarian dishes, turn to the VEGETARIAN topic on page 132 for further phrases.

The menu, please	**La carta, por favor**
	la **kar**ta, por fa-**bor**
What is the dish of the day?	**¿Cuál es el plato del día?**
	¿kwal es el **pla**-to del **dee**-a?
Do you have...?	**¿Tienen...?**
	¿**tye**-nen...?
a set-price menu	**menú del día**
	me-**noo** del **dee**-a
a children's menu	**menú para niños**
	me-**noo** pa-ra **nee**nyos
Can you recommend a local dish?	**¿Puede recomendar algún plato típico de aquí?**
	¿**pwe**-de re-ko-men-**dar** al**goon** **pla**-to **tee**-pee-ko de a-**kee**?

Querría reservar una mesa para ... personas
ke-**rree**-a re-sair-**bar oo**-na **me**-sa pa-ra ...
  pair-**so**-nas
I'd like to book a table for ... people

¿Para cuándo?
¿pa-ra **kwan**do?
When for?

**Para esta noche .../para mañana por la noche
.../a las ocho**
pa-ra **es**ta **no**-che .../pa-ra ma-**nya**-na por la
  no-che .../a las **o**-cho
for tonight .../for tomorrow night .../at 8 o'clock

What is in this?	**¿Qué lleva este plato?**
	¿ke **lye**-ba **es**te **pla**-to?
I'll have this	**Voy a tomar esto**
(point at menu)	boy a to-**mar es**to
Excuse me!	**¡Oiga, por favor!**
	¡**oy**ga, por fa-**bor**!
Please bring...	**¿Nos trae...?**
	¿nos **tra**-e...?
more bread	**más pan**
	mas pan
more water	**más agua**
	mas **a**-gwa
another bottle	**otra botella**
	o-tra bo-**te**-lya

In a restaurant

131

the bill	**la cuenta**
	la **kwen**ta
Is service included?	**¿Está incluido el servicio?**
	¿es**ta** een-kloo-**ee**-do el sair-**bee**-thyo?

Vegetarian

Don't expect great things – the Spanish love good meat!

Are there any vegetarian restaurants here?	**¿Hay algún restaurante vegetariano aquí?**
	¿**a**ee al**goon** res-tow-**ran**-te be-khe-ta-**rya**-no a-**kee**?
Do you have any vegetarian dishes?	**¿Tienen algún plato vegetariano?**
	¿**tye**-nen al**goon pla**-to be-khe-ta-**rya**-no?
Which dishes have no meat/fish?	**¿Cuáles son los platos que no llevan carne/pescado?**
	¿**kwa**-les son los **pla**-tos que no **lye**-ban **kar**ne/pes-**ka**-do?
What fish dishes do you have?	**¿Qué tienen de pescado?**
	¿ke **tye**-nen de pes-**ka**-do?

I'd like pasta as a starter	**De primero, quisiera tomar pasta**
	de pree-**me**-ro, kee-**sye**-ra to-**mar pas**ta
I don't like meat	**No me gusta la carne**
	no me **goos**ta la **kar**ne
What do you recommend?	**¿Qué me recomienda?**
	¿ke me re-ko-**myen**-da?
Is it made with vegetable stock?	**¿Está hecho con caldo de verduras?**
	¿es**ta e**-cho kon **kal**do de bair-**doo**-ras?

Possible dishes

berenjenas aubergines

ensalada salad

espárragos asparagus

gazpacho cold cucumber, peppers, garlic and tomato soup

pisto peppers, courgettes, onions cooked in a tomato sauce

judías verdes French beans

revuelto de champiñones mushrooms with scrambled eggs

revuelto de espinacas spinach with scrambled eggs

tortilla española omelette with potato and onions

133

Wines and spirits

• •

The wine list, please	**La carta de vinos, por favor**
	la **kar**ta de **bee**nos, por fa-**bor**
Can you recommend a good wine?	**¿Puede recomendar un buen vino?**
	¿**pwe**-de re-ko-men-**dar** oon bwen **bee**no?
A bottle...	**Una botella...**
	oona bo-**te**-lya...
A carafe...	**Una jarra...**
	oona **kha**-rra...
of the house wine	**de vino de la casa**
	de **bee**no de la **ka**-sa
of red wine	**de vino tinto**
	de **bee**no **teen**to
of white wine	**de vino blanco**
	de **bee**no **blan**ko

Wines
. . . .

Albariño smooth white wine from Galicia
Alella dry, medium-dry white wines from Cataluña
Alicante strong country reds and **Fondillón**, aged mature wine
Cariñena mainly red wines, best drunk young, from Aragón

Cava good quality sparkling white wine from
  Penedés (similar to Champagne)
Cigales light, fruity, dry rosé wines from
  Castilla-León
Jumilla strong, dark red wines from Murcia
Lágrima one of the best of the **Málaga** wines,
  very sweet
La Mancha firm whites and reds from Castilla-
  La Mancha
Málaga fortified, sweet, dark dessert wine
Navarra full-bodied reds from Navarra
Penedés fine reds, rosés and whites.
  Home of **Cava**
Ribeiro young, fresh, white wines from Galicia
Ribera del Duero fruity rosés and deep
  distinguished reds from the banks of the river
  Duero in Castilla-León
Rioja some of the finest red wines of Spain:
  full-bodied, rich and aged in oak. Also good white
  Riojas aged in oak
Valdepeñas soft, fruity, red wines and white wines

Types of sherry

Jerez sherry
Fino light, dry sherry, usually served chilled as
  an apéritif
Amontillado dry, nutty, amber sherry made from
  matured **fino**

Oloroso a dark, rich sherry which has been aged.
It is often sweetened and sold as a cream sherry

Palo cortado midway between an **oloroso** and
a **fino**

Other drinks

What liqueurs do you have?	¿Qué licores tienen?
	¿ke lee-**ko**-res **tye**-nen?

Anís aniseed-flavoured liqueur
Coñac Spanish brandy
Orujo strong spirit made from grape pressings
Pacharán sloe brandy
Ron rum
Sidra dry cider from Asturias

Menu reader

Drinks and tapas

There are many different varieties of **tapas** depending on the region. A larger portion of **tapas** is called a **ración**. A **pincho** is a **tapa** on a cocktail stick.

aceite oil
  aceite de oliva olive oil
aceitunas olives
  aceitunas rellenas stuffed olives
adobo, ...en marinated
agua water
  agua mineral mineral water
  agua con gas sparkling water
  agua sin gas still water
ahumado smoked
ajillo, ...al with garlic
ajo garlic
albaricoque apricot
albóndigas meatballs in sauce
alcachofas artichokes
aliño dressing

alioli/allioli olive oil and garlic mashed together into a creamy paste similar to mayonnaise. Served with meat, potatoes or fish

almejas clams

  almejas a la marinera steamed clams cooked with parsley, wine and garlic

almendras almonds

alubias large white beans found in many stews

anchoa anchovy

anguila eel

angulas baby eels, highly prized

arenque herring

arroz rice

  arroz a la cubana rice with fried egg and tomato sauce

  arroz con leche rice pudding flavoured with cinnamon

  arroz negro black rice (with squid in its own ink)

asado roasted

  asadillo roasted sliced red peppers in olive oil and garlic

atún tuna (usually fresh)

avellana hazelnut

bacalao salt cod, cod

  bacalao a la vizcaína salt cod cooked with dried peppers, onions and parsley

  bacalao al pil-pil a Basque speciality – salt cod cooked in a creamy garlic and olive oil sauce

bacalao con patatas salt cod slowly baked with
potatoes, peppers, tomatoes, onions, olives and
bay leaves

bandeja de quesos cheese platter

barbacoa, ...a la barbecued

berenjena aubergine (eggplant)

besugo red bream

bizcocho sponge

  bizcocho borracho sponge soaked in wine
and syrup

bocadillo sandwich (French bread)

  bocadillo (de...) sandwich

bogavante lobster

bonito tunny fish, lighter than tuna, good grilled

boquerones fresh anchovies

  boquerones en vinagre fresh anchovies
marinated in garlic, parsley and olive oil

  boquerones fritos fried anchovies

brasa, ...a la barbecued

buñuelos type of fritter. Savoury ones are filled
with cheese, ham, mussels or prawns. Sweet ones
can be filled with fruit

  buñuelos de bacalao salt cod fritters

butifarra special sausage from Catalonia

  butifarra blanca white sausage containing pork
and tripe

  butifarra negra black sausage containing pork
blood, belly and spices

caballa mackerel
cabrito kid (goat)
  cabrito al horno roast kid
café coffee
  café con leche white coffee
  café cortado coffee with only a little milk
  café descafeinado decaffeinated coffee
  café solo black coffee
calabacines courgettes
calabaza guisada stewed pumpkin
calamares squid
  calamares en su tinta squid cooked in its own ink
  calamares fritos fried squid
  calamares rellenos stuffed squid
caldereta stew/casserole
caldo clear soup
  caldo de pescado fish soup
  caldo gallego clear soup with green vegetables, beans, pork and **chorizo**
caliente hot
callos tripe
camarones shrimps
cangrejo crab
caracoles snails
caracolillos winkles
carajillo black coffee with brandy which may be set alight depending on regional customs
carne meat
  carne de buey beef

castaña chestnut

cazuela de fideos bean, meat and noodle stew

cebolla onion

  cebollas rellenas stuffed onions

  cebollas rojas red onions

centollo spider crab

cerdo pork

  cerdo asado roast pork

cerezas cherries

champiñones mushrooms

chilindrón, ...al sauce made with pepper, tomato, fried onions and meat (pork or lamb)

chistorra spicy sausage from Navarra

chocolate either chocolate (for eating) or a hot thick drinking chocolate: **un chocolate**

chorizo spicy red sausage. The larger type is eaten like salami, the thinner type is cooked in various dishes

chuleta chop

chuletón large steak

churrasco barbecued steak

churros fried batter sticks sprinkled with sugar, usually eaten with thick hot chocolate; in some parts of Spain they are called **porras**

cigalas king prawns

ciruelas plums

coca (coques) type of pizza with meat, fish or vegetables served in the Balearic Islands.

cochinillo roast suckling pig

cocido stew made with various meats, vegetables and chickpeas. There are regional variations of this dish and it is worth trying the local version

coco coconut

cóctel de gambas prawn cocktail

codillo de cerdo pig's trotter

codorniz quail

col cabbage

coles de Bruselas Brussels sprouts

coliflor cauliflower

conejo rabbit

consomé consommé

copa de helado ice cream sundae

cordero lamb

costillas ribs

   costillas de cerdo pork ribs

crema cream soup/cream

   crema catalana similar to crème brûlée

croquetas croquettes (made with thick bechamel sauce)

crudo raw

cuajada cream-based dessert like junket, served with honey or sugar

cucurucho de helado ice cream cone

descafeinado decaffeinated

dorada sea bream

   dorada a la sal sea bream cooked in the oven, covered only with salt, forming a crust

dorada al horno baked sea bream
dulce sweet
dulces cakes and pastries

embutido sausage, cold meat
empanada pastry/pie filled with meat or fish and vegetables
empanadilla pasty/small pie filled with meat or fish
empanado breadcrumbed and fried
ensaimada sweet spiral-shaped yeast bun from Majorca
ensalada (mixta/verde) (mixed/green) salad
  ensalada de la casa lettuce, tomato and onion salad (may include tuna)
  ensaladilla rusa potato salad with diced vegetables, hard-boiled eggs and mayonnaise
entremeses starters
escabeche, ...en pickled
escalfado poached
escalivada salad of chargrilled or baked vegetables such as peppers and aubergines soaked in olive oil
escalope de ternera veal/beef escalope
escudella meat, vegetable and chickpea stew. Traditionally served as two courses: a soup and then the cooked meat and vegetables
espárragos asparagus
esqueixada salad made with salt cod
estofado braised/stewed

fabada asturiana pork, cured ham, black pudding, large butter beans or sausage stew with **chorizo** and **morcilla**

fiambre cold meat

fideos noodles/thin ribbons of pasta (vermicelli)

filete fillet steak

  filete de ternera veal/beef steak

  filetes de lenguado sole fillets

flan crème caramel

frambuesas raspberries

fresas strawberries

frito fried

fritura de pescado fried assortment of fish

fruta fruit

frutos secos nuts

galleta biscuit

gallina hen

gambas prawns

  gambas a la plancha grilled prawns

  gambas al ajillo grilled prawns with garlic

  gambas al pil-pil sizzling prawns cooked with chillies

garbanzos chickpeas

gazpacho traditional cold tomato soup of southern Spain. There are many different recipes. Basic ingredients are water, tomatoes, garlic, fresh bread-crumbs, salt, vinegar and olive oil. Sometimes served with diced cucumber, hardboiled eggs and cured ham

gran reserva classification given to aged wines of exceptional quality

granada pomegranate

granizado/a fruit drink (usually lemon) with crushed ice

gratinado au gratin

grelos young turnip tops

guindilla chilli

guisado stew or casserole

guisantes peas

gulas a cheap alternative to **angulas**, made of fish (mainly haddock) and squid ink

habas broad beans

helado ice cream

hervido boiled

hígado liver

higos figs

horchata de chufas cool drink made with tiger (chufa) nuts

horno, ...al baked (in oven)

huevos eggs
  huevos a la flamenca baked eggs with tomatoes, peas, peppers, asparagus and **chorizo**

ibéricos traditional Spanish gourmet products; a **surtido de ibéricos** means assorted products such as cured ham, cheese, **chorizo** and **salchichón**

infusión herbal tea

jamón ham

  jamón de Jabugo Andalusian prime-quality cured ham (from Jabugo, a small town in Huelva)

  jamón serrano dark red cured ham

  jamón (de) York cooked ham

judías beans

  judías blancas haricot beans

  judías verdes green beans

jurel horse mackerel

kokotxas hake's cheek, usually fried

lacón con grelos salted pork with young turnip tops and white cabbage

langosta lobster

langostinos king prawns

leche milk

  leche frita very thick custard dipped into an egg and breadcrumb mixture, fried and served hot

lechuga lettuce

legumbres fresh or dried pulses

lengua tongue

lenguado sole

lentejas lentils (very popular in Spain)

limón lemon

lomo loin of pork

longaniza spicy pork sausage

lubina sea bass

macedonia de fruta fruit salad

maíz sweetcorn

manitas de cerdo pig's trotters

mantequilla butter

manzana apple

manzanilla camomile tea; also a very dry sherry
from Sanlúcar de Barrameda

mariscada mixed shellfish

marisco shellfish ; seafood

marmitako tuna fish and potato stew

mazapán marzipan

medallón thick steak (medallion)

mejillones mussels

melocotón peach
  melocotón en almíbar peaches in syrup

melón melon

menestra de verduras fresh vegetable stew often
cooked with cured ham

merluza hake, one of the most popular fish in Spain

mermelada jam

mero grouper

miel honey

mojama cured tuna fish, a delicacy

mojo a sauce made from olive oil, vinegar, garlic
and different spices. Paprika is added for the red
  mojo. Predominantly found in the Canaries
  mojo picón spicy **mojo** made with chilli peppers
  mojo verde made with fresh coriander

mollejas sweetbreads

morcilla black pudding
moros y cristianos rice, black beans and onions
  with garlic sausage
mostaza mustard
naranja orange
nata cream
natillas sort of custard
navajas razor clams
nécora sea crab
níspero medlar

olla stew made traditionally with white beans, beef
  and bacon
  olla gitana thick stew/soup made with chickpeas,
  pork and vegetables and flavoured with almonds
  and saffron
  olla podrida thick cured ham, vegetable and
  chickpea stew/soup
ostras oysters

paella one of the most famous of Spanish dishes.
  Paella varies from region to region but usually
  consists of rice, chicken, shellfish, vegetables,
  garlic and saffron. The traditional paella Valenciana
  contains rabbit, chicken and sometimes eel
pan bread
parrilla, ...a la grilled
pasas raisins
pastel cake/pastry

patatas potatoes
  patatas bravas fried diced potatoes mixed with a garlic, oil and vinegar dressing and flavoured with tomatoes and red chilli peppers
  patatas fritas chips/crisps
pato duck
pavo turkey
pechuga de pollo chicken breast
pepino cucumber
pepitoria de pavo/pollo turkey/chicken fricassée
pera pear
percebes goose-neck barnacles, a Galician shellfish
perdiz partridge
perejil parsley
pescado fish
pescaíto frito mixed fried fish
pez espada swordfish
pimienta pepper (spice)
pimientos red and green peppers
  pimientos de piquillo pickled red peppers
  pimientos morrones sweet red peppers
  pimientos rellenos peppers stuffed with meat or fish
piña pineapple
pinchos small tapas
  pinchos morunos pork grilled on a skewer. If you ask for a **pinchito** you can omit the word **moruno**, but if you say **pincho** you have to add **moruno**
plancha, ...a la grilled

plátano banana
pollo chicken
  pollo al chilindrón chicken cooked with onion, ham, garlic, red pepper and tomatoes
  pollo en pepitoria breaded chicken pieces casseroled with herbs, almonds, garlic and sherry
polvorones very crumbly cakes made with almonds and often eaten with a glass of **anís**
postres desserts
potaje thick soup/stew often with pork and pulses
pote thick soup with beans and sausage which has many regional variations
  pote gallego thick soup made with cabbage, white kidney beans, potatoes, pork and sausage
puchero hotpot made from meat or fish
  puchero canario salted fish and potatoes served with **mojo** sauce
puerros leeks
pulpo octopus
puré de patatas mashed potatoes

queimada warm drink made with **aguardiente** (pale brandy) sweetened with sugar and flamed, a speciality of Galicia
queso cheese
  queso de oveja mild sheep's cheese from León
  queso fresco soft fresh cheese

rabo de toro bull's tail, usually cooked in a stew

rape monkfish

rebozado in batter

rehogado lightly fried

relleno stuffed

revuelto scrambled eggs often cooked with another ingredient

riñones al jerez kidneys in sherry sauce

rodaballo turbot

romana, ...a la fried in batter (generally squid – **calamares**)

romesco sauce made traditionally with olive oil, red pepper and bread. Other ingredients are often added, such as almonds and garlic

sal salt

salchicha sausage

salchichón salami-type sausage

salmón salmon
   salmón ahumado smoked salmon

salmonete red mullet

salpicón chopped seafood or meat with tomato, onion, garlic and peppers

salsa sauce
   salsa verde garlic, olive oil and parsley sauce

salteado sautéed

sandía watermelon

sardinas sardines

sepia cuttlefish

sesos brains

setas wild mushrooms

sobrasada a paprika-flavoured pork sausage
from Mallorca

sofrito basic sauce made with slowly fried onions,
garlic and tomato

solomillo sirloin

sopa soup

  sopa de ajo garlic soup with bread. May contain
poached egg or cured ham

sorbete sorbet

tapas appetizers; snacks

tarta cake or tart

  tarta helada ice-cream cake

té tea

ternera veal/beef

tocinillo (de cielo) dessert made with egg yolk
and sugar

tocino bacon

tomates tomatoes

torrija bread dipped in milk and then fried and
sprinkled with sugar and cinnamon

tortilla (española) traditional potato and onion
omelette, often served as a tapa

trucha trout

turrón nougat

  turrón de Alicante, turrón duro hard nougat

  turrón de Jijona, turrón blando soft nougat

uvas grapes

vapor, ...al steamed
verduras vegetables
vieiras scallops
vinagre vinegar
yemas small cakes that look like egg yolks

zanahorias carrots
zarzuela de mariscos mixed seafood with wine
  and saffron
zarzuela de pescado fish stew
zumo juice
  zumo de melocotón peach juice
  zumo de naranja orange juice
  zumo de tomate tomato juice

Grammar

Nouns

• •

Unlike English, Spanish nouns have a gender: they are either masculine (**el**) or feminine (**la**). Therefore words for 'the' and 'a(n)' must agree with the noun they accompany – whether masculine, feminine or plural:

	masculine	feminine	plural
the	**el gato**	**la plaza**	**los gatos, las plazas**
a, an	**un gato**	**una plaza**	**unos gatos, unas plazas**

The ending of the noun will usually indicate whether it is masculine or feminine:

-**o** or -**or** are generally masculine
-**a**, -**dad**, -**ión**, -**tud**, -**umbre** are generally feminine

Formation of plurals

The articles **el** and **la** become **los** and **las** in the plural. Nouns ending with a vowel become plural by adding **-s**:

el gato → **los gatos**
la plaza → **las plazas**
la calle → **las calles**

If the noun ends in a consonant, **-es** is added:

el color → **los colores**
la ciudad → **las ciudades**

Nouns ending in **-z** change their ending to **-ces** in the plural:

el lápiz → **los lápices**
la voz → **las voces**

Adjectives

• •

Adjectives normally follow the nouns they describe
in Spanish, e.g. **la manzana roja** (the red apple).
Spanish adjectives also reflect the gender of the
noun they describe. To make an adjective feminine,
the masculine **-o** ending is changed to **-a**; and the
endings **-án**, **-ón**, **-or**, **-és** change to **-ana**, **-ona**,
-ora, **-esa** (adjectives ending in **-e** don't change):

masculine	feminine
el libro rojo (the red book)	**la manzana roja** (the red apple)
el hombre hablador (the talkative man)	**la mujer habladora** (the talkative woman)

To make an adjective plural an **-s** is added to the
singular form if it ends in a vowel. If the adjective
ends in a consonant, **-es** is added:

masculine	feminine
los libros rojos (the red books)	**las manzanas rojas** (the red apples)
los hombres habladores (the talkative men)	**las mujeres habladoras** (the talkative women)

My, your, his, her...

These words also depend on the gender and number of the noun they accompany and not on the sex of the 'owner'.

	with masc. sing. noun	with fem. sing. noun	with plural nouns
my	**mi**	**mi**	**mis**
your (familiar sing.)	**tu**	**tu**	**tus**
your (polite sing.)	**su**	**su**	**sus**
his/her/its	**su**	**su**	**sus**
our	**nuestro**	**nuestra**	**nuestros/ nuestras**
your (familiar pl.)	**vuestro**	**vuestra**	**vuestros/ vuestras**
your (polite pl.)	**su**	**su**	**sus**
their	**su**	**su**	**sus**

There is no distinction between 'his' and 'her' in Spanish: **su billete** can mean either his or her ticket.

Pronouns

● ●

A pronoun is a word that you use to refer to
someone or something when you do not need to
use a noun, often because the person or thing has
been mentioned earlier. Examples are 'it', 'she',
'something' and 'myself'.

subject		object	
I	**yo**	me	**me**
you (familiar sing.)	**tú**	you	**te**
you (polite sing.)	**usted (Ud.)**	you	**le**
he/it	**él**	him/it	**le, lo**
she/it	**ella**	her/it	**le, la**
we (masc.) (fem.)	**nosotros** **nosotras**	us	**nos**
you (masc.) (fem.) (familiar pl.)	**vosotros** **vosotras**	you	**os**
you (polite pl.)	**ustedes (Uds.)**	you	**les**
they (masc.) (fem.)	**ellos** **ellas**	them them	**les, los** **les, las**

Grammar

158

Subject pronouns (I, you, he, etc.) are generally omitted in Spanish, since the verb ending distinguishes the subject:

hablo   <u>I</u> speak
hablamos   <u>we</u> speak

Object pronouns are placed before the verb in Spanish:

la veo   I see <u>her</u>
los conocemos we know <u>them</u>

However, in commands or requests they follow the verb:

¡ayúdame!   help <u>me</u>!
¡escúchale!   listen to <u>him</u>!

Except when they are expressed in the negative:

¡no me ayudes!   don't help <u>me</u>!
¡no le escuches! don't listen to <u>him</u>!

The object pronouns shown above can be used to mean 'to me', 'to us', etc., but 'to him/to her' is **le** and 'to them' is **les**. If **le** and **les** occur in combinations with **lo/la/las/los** then **le/les** change to **se**, e.g. **se lo doy** (I give it to him).

Verbs

● ●

A verb is a word such as 'sing', 'walk' or 'cry' which is used with a subject to say what someone or something does or what happens to them. Regular verbs follow the same pattern of endings. Irregular verbs do not follow a regular pattern so you need to learn the different endings.

There are three main patterns of endings for Spanish verbs – those ending -**ar**, -**er** and -**ir** in the dictionary.

	cantar	**to sing**
	canto	I sing
	cantas	you sing
(usted)	**canta**	(s)he sings/you sing
	cantamos	we sing
	cantáis	you sing
(ustedes)	**cantan**	they sing/you sing

	vivir	**to live**
	vivo	I live
	vives	you live
(usted)	**vive**	(s)he lives/you live
	vivimos	we live
	vivís	you live
(ustedes)	**viven**	they live/you live

	comer	**to eat**
	como	I eat
	comes	you eat
(usted)	come	(s)he eats/you eat
	comemos	we eat
	coméis	you eat
(ustedes)	comen	they eat/you eat

In Spanish there are two ways of addressing people: the polite form (for people you don't know well or who are older) and the familiar form (for friends, family and children). The polite you is **usted** in the singular, and **ustedes** in the plural. You can see from above that **usted** uses the same verb ending as for he and she; **ustedes** the same ending as for they. Often the words **usted** and **ustedes** are omitted, but the verb ending itself indicates that you are using the polite form. The informal words for you are **tú** (singular) and **vosotros/as** (plural).

The verb 'to be'

• •

There are two different Spanish verbs for 'to be' –
ser and **estar**.

Ser is used to describe a permanent state:

soy inglés	I am English
es una playa	it is a beach

Estar is used to describe a temporary state or
where something is located:

¿cómo está?	how are you?
¿dónde está la playa?	where is the beach?

	ser	**to be**
	soy	I am
	eres	you are
(usted)	**es**	(s)he is/you are
	somos	we are
	sois	you are
(ustedes)	**son**	they are/you are

	estar	**to be**
	estoy	I am
	estás	you are
(usted)	está	(s)he is/you are
	estamos	we are
	estáis	you are
(ustedes)	están	they are/you are

Other common irregular verbs include:

	tener	**to have**
	tengo	I have
	tienes	you have
(usted)	tiene	(s)he has/you have
	tenemos	we have
	tenéis	you have
(ustedes)	tienen	they have/you have

	ir	**to go**
	voy	I go
	vas	you go
(usted)	va	(s)he goes/you go
	vamos	we go
	vais	you go
(ustedes)	van	they go/you go

Grammar

	querer	**to want**
	quiero	I want
	quieres	you want
(usted)	quiere	(s)he wants/you want
	queremos	we want
	queréis	you want
(ustedes)	quieren	they want/you want
	hacer	**to do**
	hago	I do
	haces	you do
(usted)	hace	(s)he does/you do
	hacemos	we do
	hacéis	you do
(ustedes)	hacen	they do/you do

Public holidays

• •

January 1	**Año Nuevo** New Year's Day
January 6	**Día de Reyes** Epiphany or the Adoration of the Magi
March 19	**San José/el Día del Padre** Father's Day
May 1	**Día del Trabajo** Labour Day
August 15	**La Asunción** Assumption Day
October 12	**Día de la Hispanidad** Spain's National Day
November 1	**Día de Todos los Santos** All Saints' Day
December 6	**Día de la Constitución** Constitution Day
December 8	**Día de la Inmaculada** Inmaculate Conception
December 25	**Día de Navidad** Christmas Day
Variable	**Jueves y Viernes Santo** Maundy Thursday and Good Friday

As well as the above national holidays, each town celebrates the feast-day of its patron saint, which differs from town to town.

English – Spanish

A		
a(n)	un(a)	oon/**oo**na
about (concerning)	sobre	**so**-bre
above	arriba; por encima	a-**rree**-ba; por en-**thee**-ma
abroad	en el extranjero	en el eks-tran-**khe**-ro
access	el acceso	ak-**the**-so
wheelchair access	el acceso para sillas de ruedas	
accident	el accidente	ak-thee-**den**-te
accommodation	el alojamiento	el a-lo-kha-**myen**-to
account (bank, etc)	la cuenta	**kwen**ta
account number	el número de cuenta	**noo**-me-ro de **kwen**ta
to ache	doler	do-**lair**
my head aches	me duele la cabeza	
address	la dirección	dee-rek-**thyon**

admission charge/fee	el precio de entrada	**pre**-thyo de en-**tra**-da
adult	el/la adulto(a)	a-**dool**-to(a)
advance: *in advance*	por adelantado	por a-de-lan-**ta**-do
A&E	las urgencias	oor-**khen**-thyas
after	después	des**pwes**
afternoon	la tarde	**tarde**
this afternoon	esta tarde	
in the afternoon	por la tarde	
again	otra vez	**o**-tra beth
age	la edad	e-**dad**
ago: *a week ago*	hace una semana	a-the **oo**na se-**ma**-na
air conditioning	el aire acondicionado	**aee**-re a-kon-dee-thyo-**na**-do
airplane	el avión	a-**byon**
airport	el aeropuerto	a-e-ro-**pwair**-to

English	Spanish	pronunciation
airport bus	el autobús del aeropuerto	ow-to-**boos** del a-e-ro-**pwair**-to
air ticket	el billete de avión	bee-**lye**-te de a-**byon**
alarm	la alarma	a-**lar**-ma
alarm clock	el despertador	des-pair-ta-**dor**
alcohol	el alcohol	al**kol**
alcohol-free	sin alcohol	seen al**kol**
all	todo(a)/ todos(as)	**to**-do(a)/ **to**-dos(as)
allergic to	alérgico(a) a	a-**lair**-khee-ko(a) a
I'm allergic to...	soy alérgico(a) a...	
allergy	la alergia	a-**lair**-khya
all right (agreed) (OK)	de acuerdo vale	de a-**kwair**-do **ba**-le
are you all right?	¿está bien?	
alone	solo(a)	**so**-lo(a)
already	ya	ya
also	también	tam**byen**
always	siempre	**syem**pre

English	Spanish	pronunciation
a.m.	de la mañana	de la ma-**nya**-na
ambulance	la ambulancia	am-boo-**lan**-thya
America	Norteamérica	nor-te-a-**me**-ree-ka
American	norte americano(a)	nor-te-a-me-ree-**ka**-no(a)
anaesthetic	la anestesia	a-nes-**te**-sya
and	y	ee
angina	la angina (de pecho)	an-**khee**-na (de **pe**-cho)
angry	enfadado(a)	en-fa-**da**-do(a)
another	otro(a)	**o**-tro(a)
answer	la respuesta	res-**pwes**-ta
to answer	responder	res-pon-**dair**
antibiotic	el antibiótico	an-tee-**byo**-tee-ko
antihistamine	el antihistamínico	an-tee-eesta-**mee**-nee-ko
antiseptic	el antiséptico	an-tee-**sep**-tee-ko
any	alguno(a)	al-**goo**-no(a)
anyone	alguien	al**gyen**

166|167

English – Spanish

English	Spanish	pronunciation
anything	algo	algo
apartment	el apartamento	a-par-ta-**men**-to
apple	la manzana	man-**tha**-na
apricot	el albaricoque	al-ba-ree-**ko**-ke
April	abril	a**breel**
arm	el brazo	**bra**-tho
to arrest	detener	de-te-**nair**
arrivals (plane, train)	las llegadas	lye-**ga**-das
to arrive	llegar	lye-**gar**
art	el arte	**arte**
to ask (question)	preguntar	pre-goon-**tar**
(ask for something)	pedir	pe-**deer**
aspirin	la aspirina	as-pee-**ree**-na
asthma	el asma	**asma**
I have asthma	tengo asma	
at	a; en	a; en
at home	en casa	en **ka**-sa
at 8 o'clock	a las ocho	
at night	por la noche	
to attack	atacar	a-ta-**kar**

English	Spanish	pronunciation
August	agosto	a-**gos**-to
Australia	Australia	ows-**tra**-lya
Australian	australiano(a)	ows-tra-**lya**-no(a)
autumn	el otoño	o-**to**-nyo
available	disponible	dees-po-**nee**-ble
away; far away	lejos	**le**-khos
B		
baby	el bebé	be-**be**
baby food	los potitos	po-**tee**-tos
baby milk	la leche infantil	**le**-che een-fan-**teel**
babyseat (in car)	el asiento del bebé	a-**syen**-to del be-**be**
baby wipes	las toallitas infantiles	twa-**lyee**-tas een-fan-**tee**-les
back (of body)	la espalda	es-**pal**-da
bad (weather, news)	mal/malo(a)	mal/**ma**-lo(a)
(fruit and veg.)	podrido(a)	po-**dree**-do(a)
bag	la bolsa	**bol**sa

English	Spanish	Pronunciation
baggage	el equipaje	e-kee-pa-khe
baker's	la panadería	pa-na-de-ree-a
banana	el plátano	pla-ta-no
bank	el banco	ban-ko
bank account	la cuenta bancaria	kwenta ban-ka-rya
banknote	el billete	bee-lye-te
bar	el bar	bar
bath	el baño	ba-nyo
bathroom	el cuarto de baño	kwar-to de ba-nyo
battery (radio, in car)	la pila; la batería	peela; ba-te-ree-a
B&B (guesthouse)	la pensión	pen-syon
to be	estar; ser	estar; sair
beach	la playa	pla-ya
beautiful	hermoso(a)	air-mo-so(a)
because	porque	porke
bed	la cama	ka-ma
bed and breakfast	alojamiento y desayuno	a-lo-kha-myen-to ee de-sa-yoo-no
bedroom	el dormitorio	dor-mee-to-ryo
beer	la cerveza	thair-be-tha
before	antes de	antes de
to begin	empezar	em-pe-thar
behind	detrás de	de-tras de
below	por debajo de; por debajo	de-ba-kho; por de-ba-kho
beside (next to)	al lado de	al la-do de
beside the bank	al lado del banco	
best	el/la mejor	me-khor
better	mejor	me-khor
better than	mejor que	
between	entre	entre
bicycle	la bicicleta	bee-thee-kle-ta
by bicycle	en bicicleta	
big	grande	grande
bigger than	mayor que	
bill	la factura	fak-too-ra
(in restaurant)	la cuenta	kwenta
birthday	el cumpleaños	koom-ple-a-nyos
biscuits	las galletas	ga-lye-tas

English – Spanish

English – Spanish

English	Spanish	Pronunciation
bit: *a bit of*	un poco de	oon **po**-ko de
bite (insect)	la picadura	pee-ka-**doo**-ra
(animal)	la mordedura	mor-de-**doo**-ra
black	negro(a)	**ne**-gro(a)
to bleed	sangrar	sangrar
blind (person)	ciego(a)	thye-go(a)
blond (person)	rubio(a)	**roo**byo(a)
blood	la sangre	sangre
blood group	el grupo sanguíneo	**groo**po san-**gee**-ne-o
blood pressure	la presión sanguínea	pre-**syon** san-**gee**-ne-a
blood test	el análisis de sangre	a-**na**-lee-sees de sangre
blouse	la blusa	**bloo**sa
blue	azul	a-**thool**
to board (train, etc)	subir	soo**beer**
boarding card/ pass	la tarjeta de embarque	tar-**khe**-ta de em-**bar**-ke
body	el cuerpo	**kwair**po
to boil	hervir	air**beer**
book	el libro	**lee**bro
to book	reservar	re-sair-**bar**
booking	la reserva	re-**sair**-ba
booking office (train)	la ventanilla de billetes	ben-ta-**nee**-lya de **bee**-lye-tes
bookshop	la librería	lee-bre-**ree**-a
boots	las botas	**bo**-tas
both	ambos(as)	**ambos(as)**
bottle	la botella	bo-**te**-lya
bottle opener	el abrebotellas	a-bre-bo-**te**-lyas
box office	la taquilla	ta-**kee**-lya
boy	el chico	**cheek**o
boyfriend	el novio	**no**-byo
brake	el freno	**fre**-no
to brake	frenar	fre-**nar**
brand (make)	la marca	**mar**ka
bread	el pan	pan
to break	romper	rom**pair**
breakfast	el desayuno	desa-**yoo**-no
breast	el pecho	**pe**-cho
bride	la novia	**no**-bya

English	Spanish		
bridegroom	el novio	no-byo	
briefcase	la cartera	kar-**tair**-a	
to bring	traer	tra-**air**	
Britain	Gran Bretaña	gran bre-**ta**-nya	
British	británico(a)	bree-**tan**-ee-ko(a)	
brochure	el folleto	fo-**lye**-to	
broken	roto(a)	**ro**-to(a)	
broken down (car, etc)	averiado(a)	a-be-**rya**-do(a)	
bronchitis	la bronquitis	bron-**kee**-tees	
brother	el hermano	air-**ma**-no	
brown	marrón	ma-**rron**	
buffet car	el coche comedor	**ko**-che ko-me-**dor**	
to build	construir	kons-troo-**eer**	
bulb (electric)	la bombilla	bom-**bee**-lya	
bureau de change	la oficina de cambio	o-fee-**thee**-na de **kam**-byo	
burger	la hamburguesa	am-boor-**ge**-sa	
bus	el autobús	ow-to-**boos**	
bus pass	el bonobús	bo-no-**boos**	
bus station	la estación de autobuses	es-ta-**thyon** de ow-to-**boo**-ses	
bus stop	la parada de autobús	pa-**ra**-da de ow-to-**boos**	
bus ticket	el billete de autobús	bee-**lye**-te de ow-to-**boos**	
business	el negocio	ne-**go**-thyo	
on business	de negocios		
businessman/ woman	el hombre/ la mujer de negocios	**ombre**/ moo**khair** de ne-**go**-thyos	
business trip	el viaje de negocios	**bya**-khe de ne-**go**-thyos	
busy	ocupado(a)	o-koo-**pa**-do(a)	
but	pero	**pe**-ro	
butcher's	la carnicería	kar-nee-the-**ree**-a	
butter	la mantequilla	man-te-**kee**-lya	
to buy	comprar	kom**prar**	
by (via)	por	por	
(beside)	al lado de	al **la**-do de	
by air	en avión		

English – Spanish

English	Spanish	Pronunciation
by bus	en autobús	
by car	en coche	
by train	en tren	
by ship	en barco	
C		
café	el café	ka-**fe**
cake	el pastel	pastel
call (telephone)	la llamada	lya-**ma**-da
to call	llamar	lya-**mar**
(phone)	llamar por teléfono	lya-**mar** por te-**le**-fo-no
camcorder	la videocámara	bee-de-o-**ka**-ma-ra
camera	la cámara	**ka**-ma-ra
to camp	acampar	a-kam-**par**
campsite	el camping	**kam**-peen
can (to be able)	poder	po-**dair**
Canada	(el) Canadá	ka-na-**da**
Canadian	canadiense	ka-na-**dyen**-se
to cancel	anular; cancelar	a-noo-**lar**; kan-the-**lar**
cancellation	la cancelación	kan-the-la-**thyon**
car	el coche	**ko**-che
car alarm	la alarma de coche	a-**lar**-ma de **ko**-che
car hire	el alquiler de coches	al-kee-**lair** de **ko**-ches
car insurance	el seguro del coche	se-**goo**-ro del **ko**-che
car keys	las llaves del coche	**lya**-bes del **ko**-che
car park	el aparcamiento	a-par-ka-**myen**-to
card (greetings, business)	la tarjeta	tar-**khe**-ta
to carry	llevar	lye-**bar**
case (suitcase)	la maleta	ma-**le**-ta
cash	el dinero en efectivo	dee-**ne**-ro en e-**fek-tee**-bo
to cash (cheque)	cobrar	ko-**brar**
cash desk	la caja	**ka**-kha
cash dispenser	el cajero automático	ka-**khe**-ro ow-to-**ma**-tee-ko

English	Spanish	Pronunciation
cashier	el/la cajero(a)	ka-**khe**-ro(a)
castle	el castillo	kas-**tee**-lyo
cat	el gato	**ga**-to
to catch (bus, etc)	coger	ko-**khair**
cathedral	la catedral	ka-te-**dral**
Catholic	católico(a)	ka-**to**-lee-ko(a)
cent	el céntimo	**then**-tee-mo
central	central	then**tral**
central heating	la calefacción central	ka-**to**-lee-ko(a) then**tral**
centre	el centro	**then**tro
cereal	los cereales	the-re-**a**-les
chair	la silla	**see**lya
chalet	el chalet	cha-**let**
change	el cambio	**kam**byo
(small coins)	el suelto	**swel**to
(money returned)	la vuelta	**bwel**ta
to change	cambiar	kam-**byar**
(clothes)	cambiarse	kam-**byar**-se
(train)	hacer transbordo	a-**thair** trans-**bor**-do
to change money	cambiar dinero	
charge (fee)	el precio	**pre**-thyo
(electrical)	la carga	**kar**ga
to charge (money)	cobrar	ko-**brar**
(battery)	cargar	**kar**gar
cheap	barato(a)	ba-**ra**-to(a)
to check	revisar; comprobar	re-bee-**sar**; kom-pro-**bar**
to check in (at airport)	facturar el equipaje	fak-too-**rar** e-kee-**pa**-khe
(at hotel)	registrarse	re-khees-**trar**-se
check-in	la facturación	fak-too-ra-**thyon**
cheers!	¡salud!	¡sa-**lood**!
cheese	el queso	**ke**-so
chef	el chef	chef
chemist's	la farmacia	far-**ma**-thya
cheque	el cheque	**che**-ke
cheque book	el talonario	ta-lo-**na**-ryo
cherry	la cereza	the-**re**-tha
chicken	el pollo	**po**-lyo
child boy/girl	el niño/la niña	**nee**nyo/ **nee**nya

English – Spanish

English – Spanish

children (infants)	los niños	**neen**yos	clock	el reloj	re-**lokh**
chips	las patatas fritas	pa-**ta**-tas **free**tas	to close	cerrar	the-**rrar**
			closed (shop, etc)	cerrado(a)	the-**rra**-do(a)
chocolate	el chocolate	cho-ko-**la**-te	clothes	la ropa	**ro**-pa
chocolates	los bombones	bom-**bo**-nes	clothes shop	la tienda de ropa	**tyenda** de **ro**-pa
Christmas	la Navidad	na-bee-**dad**	cloudy	nublado(a)	noo-**bla**-do(a)
Christmas Eve	la Nochebuena	no-che-**bwe**-na	coach (bus)	el autocar	ow-to-**kar**
church	la iglesia	ee-**gle**-sya	coast	la costa	**kos**ta
cigarette	el cigarrillo	thee-ga-**rree**-lyo	coat	el abrigo	a-**bree**-go
cigarette lighter	el mechero	me-**che**-ro	coffee	el café	ka-**fe**
			coin	la moneda	mo-**ne**-da
cinema	el cine	**thee**ne	cold	frío(a)	**free**-o(a)
city	la ciudad	thyoo**dad**	I'm cold	tengo frío	
city centre	el centro de la ciudad	**thent**ro de la thyoo**dad**	it's cold	hace frío	
			cold (illness)	el resfriado	res-free-**a**-do
			I have a cold	estoy resfriado(a)	
class: first class	primera clase		to come	venir	be-**neer**
second class	segunda clase		(to arrive)	llegar	lye-**gar**
clean	limpio(a)	**leem**pyo(a)	to come back	volver	bolbair
to clean	limpiar	leem**pyar**	to come in	entrar	en**trar**
clear	claro(a)	**kla**-ro(a)	come in!	¡pase!	
client	el/la client(a)	klee-**en**-te(a)			

English	Spanish	pronunciation
comfortable	cómodo(a)	**ko**-mo-do(a)
company (firm)	la empresa	em-**pre**-sa
to complain	reclamar	re-kla-**mar**
complaint	la reclamación; la queja	re-kla-ma-**thyon**; **ke**-kha
computer	el ordenador	or-de-na-**dor**
concert	el concierto	kon-**thyair**-to
concert hall	la sala de conciertos	**sa**-la de kon-**thyair**-tos
conditioner	el suavizante	swa-bee-**than**-te
condom	el condón	kon**don**
conductor (on bus)	el/la cobrador(a)	el/la ko-bra-**dor**(a)
(on train)	el/la revisor(a)	re-bee-**sor**(a)
conference	el congreso	kon-**gre**-so
to confirm	confirmar	kon-feer-**mar**
confirmation (flight; booking)	la confirmación	kon-feer-ma-**thyon**
connection	el enlace	en-**la**-the
consulate	el consulado	kon-soo-**la**-do
to contact	ponerse en contacto con	po-**nair**-se en kon-**tak**-to kon
contact lens	la lentilla	len-**tee**-lya
to continue	continuar	kon-tee-**nwar**
contraceptive	el anticonceptivo	an-tee-kon-thep-**tee**-bo
contract	el contrato	kon-**tra**-to
to cook	cocinar	ko-thee-**nar**
cooked	preparado(a)	pre-pa-**ra**-do(a)
cooker	la cocina	ko-**thee**-na
corner	la esquina	es-**kee**-na
corridor	el pasillo	pa-**see**-lyo
cosmetics	los cosméticos	kos-**me**-tee-kos
cost (price)	el precio	**pre**-thyo
to cost	costar	kos**tar**
how much does it cost?	¿cuánto cuesta?	
costume (swim.)	el bañador	ba-nya-**dor**
cough	la tos	tos
to cough	toser	to-**sair**
country (nation)	el país	pa-**ees**
couple (2 people)	la pareja	pa-re-**kha**
course (of study)	el curso	**koor**so

English – Spanish

(of meal)	el plato	**pla**-to		
cover charge (in restaurant)	el cubierto	koo-**byair**-to		
crafts	la artesanía	ar-te-sa-**nee**-a	**daily** (each day)	cada día; diario	**ka**-da dee-a; dee-**a**-ryo
crash (car)	el accidente	ak-thee-**den**-te	**dairy produce**	los productos lácteos	pro-**dook**-tos **lak**-te-os
cream (lotion)	la crema	**kre**-ma	**damage**	el/los daño(s)	**da**-nyo(s)
(on milk)	la nata	**na**-ta	**danger**	el peligro	pe-**lee**-gro
credit card	la tarjeta de crédito	tar-**khe**-ta de **kre**-dee-to	**dangerous**	peligroso(a)	pe-lee-**gro**-so(a)
crisps	las patatas fritas	pa-**ta**-tas **free**-tas	**dark**	oscuro(a)	os-**koo**-ro(a)
			date	la fecha	**fe**-cha
to cross (road)	cruzar	kroo**thar**	**date of birth**	la fecha de nacimiento	**fe**-cha de na-thee-**myen**-to
crossroads	el cruce	**kroo**the	**daughter**	la hija	**ee**kha
to cry (weep)	llorar	lyo-**rar**	**day**	el día	**dee**-a
cup	la taza	**ta**-tha	**every day**	todos los días	
customer	el/la cliente(a)	klee-**en**-te(a)	**deaf**	sordo(a)	**sordo**(a)
customs (control)	la aduana	a-doo-**a**-na	**debt**	la deuda	**deoo**-da
to cut	cortar	eer**tar**	**debit card**	la tarjeta de débito	tar-**khe**-ta de **de**-bee-to
to cycle	ir en bicicleta	bee-thee-**kle**-ta	**December**	diciembre	dee-**thyem**-bre
cystitis	la cistitis	thees-**tee**-tees	**to declare**	declarar	de-kla-**rar**

English	Spanish	
nothing to declare	nada que declarar	
deep	profundo(a)	pro-**foon**-do(a)
delay	el retraso	re-**tra**-so
delayed	retrasado(a)	re-tra-**sa**-do(a)
dentist	el/la dentista	den-**tees**-ta
deodorant	el desodorante	de-so-do-**ran**-te
department (gen)	el departamento	de-par-ta-**men**-to
(in shop)	la sección	sek**thyon**
department store	los grandes almacenes	**gran**des al-ma-**the**-nes
departure lounge	la sala de embarque	**sa**-la de em-**bar**-ke
dessert	el postre	**postre**
details (personal)	los detalles los datos personales	de-**ta**-lyes **da**-tos pair-so-**na**-les
to develop (photos)	revelar	re-be-**lar**
diabetic	diabético(a)	dya-**be**-tee-ko(a)

English	Spanish	
I'm diabetic	soy diabético(a)	soy dya-be-tee-ko(a)
to dial	marcar	mar**kar**
dialling code	el prefijo	pre-**fee**-kho
dialling tone	el tono de marcado	**to**-no de mar-**ka**-do
diesel	el diesel; el gasóleo; el gasoil	**dye**-sel; ga-**so**-le-o; ga-**soyl**
diet	la dieta	**dye**-ta
I'm on a diet	estoy a dieta	dees-**teen**-to(a)
different	distinto(a)	dee-**fee**-theel
difficult	difícil	dee-**fee**-theel
digital camera	la cámara digital	**ka**-ma-ra dee-khee-**tal**
dining room	el comedor	ko-me-**dor**
dinner (evening meal)	la cena	**the**-na
to have dinner	cenar	the-**nar**
direct (train, etc)	directo(a)	dee-**rek**-to(a)
directions (instructions)	las instrucciones	een-strook-**thyo**-nes

176 | 177

English – Spanish

English – Spanish

English	Spanish	Pronunciation
to ask for directions	preguntar el camino	
directory (phone)	la guía telefónica	**gee**-a te-le-**fo**-nee-ka
dirty	sucio(a)	**soothy**o(a)
disabled	discapacitado(a)	dees-ka-pa-thee-**ta**-do(a)
disco	la discoteca	dees-ko-**te**-ka
discount	el descuento	des-**kwen**-to
to discover	descubrir	des-koo-**breer**
disease	la enfermedad	en-fair-me-**dad**
distance	la distancia	dees-**tan**-thya
district	el barrio	**ba**-rryo
diversion	el desvío	des-**bee**-o
divorced	divorciado(a)	dee-bor-**thya**-do(a)
dizzy	mareado(a)	ma-re-**a**-do(a)
to do	hacer	a-**thair**
doctor	el/la médico(a)	**me**-dee-ko(a)
documents	los documentos	do-koo-**men**-tos
dog	el perro	**pe**-rro

English	Spanish	Pronunciation
dollar	el dólar	**do**-lar
door	la puerta	**pwair**ta
double	doble	**do**-ble
double room	la habitación doble	a-bee-ta-**thyon do**-ble
down: to go down	bajar	ba-**khar**
downstairs	abajo	a-**ba**-kho
draught lager	la cerveza de barril	thair-**be**-tha de ba-**rreel**
dress	el vestido	bes-**tee**-do
drink	la bebida	be-**bee**-da
to drink	beber	be-**bair**
drinking water	el agua potable	a-gwa po-**ta**-ble
to drive	conducir	kon-doo-**theer**
driver	el/la conductor(a)	kon-dook-**tor**(a)
driving licence	el carné de conducir	kar-**ne** de kon-doo-**theer**
to drown	ahogarse	a-o-**gar**-se
drug	la droga	**dro**-ga
(medicine)	la medicina	me-dee-**thee**-na

drunk	borracho(a)	bo-**rra**-cho(a)
dry	seco(a)	**se**-ko(a)
to dry	secar	se-**kar**
during	durante	doo-**ran**-te
duty-free	libre de impuestos	**lee**bre de eem-**pwes**-tos
DVD player	el reproductor de DVD	re-pro-dook-**tor** de de-**oobe**-**de**

E

ear (outside)	la oreja	o-**re**-kha
(inside)	el oído	el o-**ee**-do
earache	el dolor de oído(s)	do-**lor** de o-**ee**-do(s)
earlier	antes	**an**tes
early	temprano	tem-**pra**-no
to earn	ganar	ga-**nar**
east	el este	**es**te
Easter	la Pascua; la Semana Santa	**pas**-kwa; se-**ma**-na **san**ta
easy	fácil	**fa**-theel

to eat	comer	ko-**mair**
egg	el huevo	**we**-bo
elastoplast®	la tirita	tee-**ree**-ta
electric	eléctrico(a)	e-**lek**-tree-ko(a)
electrician	el/la electricista	e-lek-tree-**thees**-ta
electricity	la electricidad	e-lek-tree-thee-**dad**
electronic	electrónico(a)	e-lek-**tro**-nee-ko(a)
e-mail	el email	ee**meyl**
e-mail address	el email	ee**meyl**
embassy	la embajada	em-ba-**kha**-da
emergency	la emergencia	e-mair-**khen**-thya
emergency exit	la salida de emergencia	sa-**lee**-da de e-mair-**khen**-thya
empty	vacío(a)	ba-**thee**-o(a)
end	el fin	feen
engaged (to marry)	prometido(a)	pro-me-**tee**-do(a)
(toilet, phone)	ocupado(a)	o-koo-**pa**-do(a)
England	Inglaterra	een-gla-**te**-rra

English – Spanish

English	Spanish	
(language)	inglés/inglesa el inglés	eengles/ een-gle-sa eengles
to enjoy (to like)	gustar	goostar
enjoy your meal!	¡qué aproveche!	
enough	bastante	bas-tan-te
enquiry desk	la información	een-for-ma-thyon
to enter	entrar en	en-tra-da
entrance	la entrada	en-tra-da
entrance fee	el precio de entrada	pre-thyo de la en-tra-da
to escape	escapar	es-ka-par
euro	el euro	eoo-ro
Europe	Europa	eoo-ro-pa
European	el/la europeo(a)	eoo-ro-pe-o(a)
European Union	la Unión Europea	oonyon eoo-ro-pe-a
evening	la tarde	tarde
every	cada	ka-da
everyone	todo el mundo; todos	to-do el moondo; to-dos

English – finish

English	Spanish	
everything	todo	to-do
everywhere	en todas partes	en to-das partes
for example:	por ejemplo	por e-khem-plo
excellent	excelente	eks-the-len-te
to exchange	cambiar	kambyar
exchange rate	el tipo de cambio	teepo de kambyo
excuse me!	¡perdón!	¡pairdon!
exercise	el ejercicio	e-khair-thee-thyo
exit	la salida	sa-lee-da
expensive	caro(a)	ka-ro(a)
to expire (ticket, etc)	caducar	ka-doo-kar
to explain	explicar	eks-plee-kar
to export	exportar	eks-por-tar
extra (in addition) (more)	de más extra	de mas ekstra
eye	el ojo	o-kho

F

English	Spanish	Pronunciation
face	la cara	ka-ra
facilities	las instalaciones	eens-ta-la-**thyo**-nes
to faint	desmayarse	des-ma-**yar**-se
fair (hair)	rubio(a)	**roo**byo(a)
(just)	justo(a)	**khoos**to(a)
fake	falso(a)	**fal**so(a)
to fall	caer;	ka-**air**;
	caerse	ka-**air**-se
family	la familia	fa-**mee**-lya
famous	famoso(a)	fa-**mo**-so(a)
fan (electric)	el ventilador	ben-tee-la-**dor**
(hand-held)	el abanico	a-ba-**nee**-ko
far	lejos	**le**-khos
fast	rápido(a)	**ra**-pee-do(a)
to fasten	abrocharse	a-bro-**char**-se
fat (plump)	gordo(a)	**gor**do(a)
(in food, on person)	la grasa	**gra**-sa
father	el padre	**pa**-dre
fault (defect)	el defecto	de-**fek**-to

English	Spanish	Pronunciation
favour	el favor	fa-**bor**
fax	el fax	faks
by fax	por fax	por faks
to fax	mandar por fax	man**dar** por faks
February	febrero	fe-**bre**-ro
to feed	dar de comer	dar de ko-**mair**
to feel	sentir	sen**teer**
I don't feel well	no me siento bien	
female	mujer	mookhair
fever	la fiebre	**fye**-bre
few	pocos(as)	**po**-kos(as)
a few	algunos(as)	
to fill	llenar	lye-**nar**
to fill in (form)	rellenar	re-lye-**nar**
fillet	el filete	fee-**le**-te
film (at cinema)	la película	pe-**lee**-koo-la
(for camera)	el carrete	ka-**rre**-te
to find	encontrar	en-kon-**trar**
fine (to be paid)	la multa	**mool**ta
finger	el dedo	**de**-do
to finish	acabar	a-ka-**bar**

English – Spanish

English - Spanish

finished	terminado(a)	tair-mee-**na**-do(a)
fire (flames)	el fuego	**fwe**-go
(blaze)	el incendio	een-**then**-dyo
fire!	¡fuego!	
fire alarm	la alarma de	a-**lar**-ma de
	incendios	een-**then**-dyos
fire exit	la salida de	sa-**lee**-da de
	incendios	een-**then**-dyos
firm (company)	la empresa	em-**pre**-sa
first	primero(a)	pree-**me**-ro(a)
first aid	los primeros	pree-**me**-ros
	auxilios	ow-**see**-lyos
first class	de primera	de pree-**mair**-a
	clase	**kla**-se
first name	el nombre	**nom**-bre de
	de pila	**pee**-la
fish (food)	el pescado	pes-**ka**-do
	peth	
(alive)	el pez	pes-**kar**
to fish	pescar	a-**ta**-ke
fit (seizure)	el ataque	ke-**dar** byen
to fit (clothes)	quedar bien	

to fix	arreglar	a-rre-**glar**
can you fix it?	¿puede arreglarlo?	
fizzy	con gas	kon gas
flat (apartment)	el piso	**pee**so
flat (battery)	llano(a)	**lya**-no(a)
flavour	descargado(a)	des-kar-**ga**-do(a)
flight	el sabor	sa-**bor**
floor (of building)	el vuelo	**bwe**-lo
(of room)	el piso	**pee**so
flower	el suelo	**swe**-lo
flu	la flor	flor
to fly	la gripe	**gree**pe
fog	volar	bo-**lar**
to fold	la niebla	**nye**-bla
to follow	doblar	do-**blar**
food	seguir	se-**geer**
food poisoning	la comida	ko-**mee**-da
	la intoxicación	een-tok-see-
	por alimentos	ka-**thyon** por
		a-lee-**men**-tos
foot	el pie	pye

English	Spanish	Pronunciation
on foot	a pie	
for	para; por	**para; por**
forbidden	prohibido(a)	pro-ee-**bee**-do(a)
foreigner	el/la extranjero(a)	eks-tran-**khe**-ro(a)
forever	para siempre	pa-ra **syem**-pre
to forget	olvidar	ol-bee-**dar**
fork (for eating)	el tenedor	te-ne-**dor**
form (document)	el impreso	eem-**pre**-so
fortnight	quince días	keen the **dee**-as
forward	adelante	a-de-**lan**-te
fountain	la fuente	**fwen**te
fracture	la fractura	frak-**tu**-ra
free (not occupied)	libre	**lee**bre
free (not costing anything)	gratis	**gra**-tees
fresh	fresco(a)	**fres**ko(a)
Friday	el viernes	**byair**nes
fried	frito(a)	**free**to(a)
friend	el/la amigo(a)	a-**mee**-go(a)
from	de; desde	de; **des**de
from Scotland	de Escocia	

English	Spanish	Pronunciation
from England	de Inglaterra	
front	la parte delantera	de-lan-**te**-ra
in front of	delante de	
fruit	la fruta	**froo**ta
to fry	freir	fre-**eer**
fuel (petrol)	la gasolina	ga-so-**lee**-na
full	lleno(a)	**lye**-no(a)
full (occupied)	ocupado(a)	o-koo-**pa**-do(a)
full board	pensión completa	pen**syon** kom-**ple**-ta
furnished	amueblado(a)	a-mwe-**bla**-do(a)

G

English	Spanish	Pronunciation
game	el juego	**khwe**-go
game (animal)	la caza	**ka**-tha
garage (for repairs)	el garaje	ga-**ra**-khe
garage (for repairs)	el taller	ta-**lyair**
garden	el jardín	khar**deen**
gate (airport)	la puerta	**pwair**ta

182 | 183

English – Spanish

English – Spanish

English	Spanish	Pronunciation
gay (person)	gay	gey
gents (toilet)	los servicios de caballeros	sair-**bee**-thyos de ka-ba-**lye**-ros
to get (to obtain)	conseguir	kon-se-**geer**
(to receive)	recibir	re-thee-**beer**
(to bring)	traer	tra-**air**
to get in/on	subir (al)	soo**beer** (al)
to get out/off	bajarse de	ba-**khar**-se de
gift	el regalo	re-**ga**-lo
gift shop	la tienda de regalos	**tyen**da de re-**ga**-los
girl	la chica	**chee**ka
girlfriend	la novia	**no**-bya
to give	dar	dar
to give back	devolver	de-bol-**bair**
glass (for drinking)	el vaso	**ba**-so
(substance)	el cristal	kreest**al**
glasses (spectacles)	las gafas	**ga**-fas
to go	ir	eer
to go back	volver	bol**bair**

English	Spanish	Pronunciation
to go in	entrar (en)	en**trar** (en)
to go out	salir	sa-**leer**
good	bueno(a)	**bwe**-no(a)
good afternoon	buenas tardes	**bwe**-nas **tar**des
grandchild	el/la nieto(a)	nye-to(a)
grandparents	los abuelos	a-**bwe**-los
grapes	las uvas	**oo**bas
great (big)	grande	**grande**
great (wonderful)	estupendo(a)	es-too-**pen**-do(a)
Great Britain	Gran Bretaña	gran bre-**tan**-ya
grey	gris	grees
group	el grupo	**groo**po
guest	el/la invitado(a)	een-bee-**ta**-do(a)
(in hotel)	el/la huésped	**wes**ped
guesthouse	la pensión	pen**syon**
guide (tour guide)	el/la guía	**gee**-a
to guide	guiar	gee-**ar**
guidebook	la guía turística	**gee**-a too-**rees**-tee-ka
guided tour	la visita con guía	bee-**see**-ta kon **gee**-a

H

English	Spanish	Pronunciation
hair	el pelo	**pe**-lo
hairdresser	el/la peluquero(a)	pe-loo-**ke**-ro(a)
half	medio(a)	**me**-dyo(a)
half an hour	media hora	
half board	media pensión	a mee-**tad** de
half-price	a mitad de precio	**pre**-thyo
ham	el jamón	kha-**mon**
hand	la mano	**ma**-no
handbag	el bolso	**bol**so
hand luggage	el equipaje de mano	e-kee-**pa**-khe de **ma**-no
hand-made	hecho(a) a mano	**e**-cho(a) a **ma**-no
hard	duro(a)	**doo**ro(a)
(difficult)	difícil	dee-**fee**-theel
to have	tener	te-**nair**
to have to	tener que	te-**nair** ke
he	él	el
head	la cabeza	ka-**be**-tha

English	Spanish	Pronunciation
health	la salud	sa-**lood**
healthy	sano(a)	**sa**-no(a)
to hear	oir	o-**eer**
heart	el corazón	ko-ra-**thon**
heating	la calefacción	ka-le-fak-**thyon**
heavy	pesado(a)	pe-**sa**-do(a)
height	la altura	al-**too**-ra
hello	hola	**o**-la
(on phone)	diga(me)	**deega**(me)
to help	ayudar	a-yoo-**dar**
here	aquí	a-**kee**
hi!	¡hola!	**io**-la!
high	alto(a)	**alto**(a)
him	él	el
hire (bike, boat, etc)	el alquiler	al-kee-**lair**
to hire	alquilar	al-kee-**lar**
hired car	el coche de alquiler	**ko**-che de al-kee-**lair**
historic	histórico(a)	ees-**to**-ree-ko(a)
to hold	tener	te-**nair**
(to contain)	contener	kon-te-**nair**

English – Spanish

English - Spanish

English	Spanish	Pronunciation
hold-up (traffic jam)	el atasco	a-**tas**-ko
holiday	las vacaciones	ba-ka-**thyo**-nes
(public)	la fiesta de vacaciones	**fye**sta
home	la casa	**ka**-sa
at home	en casa	
homosexual	homosexual	o-mo-sek-**swal**
hospital	el hospital	os-pee-**tal**
hostel	el hostal	os-**tal**
hot	caliente	ka-**lyen**-te
hour	la hora	**o**-ra
half an hour	media hora	
house	la casa	**ka**-sa
house wine	el vino de la casa	**bee**no de la **ka**-sa
how (in what way)?	cómo	**ko**-mo
how much?	¿cuánto?	
how many?	¿cuántos?	
hungry: to be hungry	tener hambre	te-**nair am**bre
hurry: I'm in a hurry	tengo prisa	**ten**go **pree**sa
to hurt (injure)	hacer daño	a-**thair da**-nyo
husband	el marido	ma-**ree**-do

I

English	Spanish	Pronunciation
I	yo	yo
ice	el hielo	**ye**-lo
(cube)	el cubito	koo-**bee**-to
icecream	el helado	e-**la**-do
iced tea	el té helado	te-**la**-do
identity card	el carné de identidad	karne de ee-den-tee-**dad**
if	si	see
ill	enfermo(a)	en-**fair**-mo(a)
illness	la enfermedad	en-fair-me-**dad**
immediately	en seguida	en se-**gee**-da
to import	importar	eem-por-**tar**
important	importante	eem-por-**tan**-te
impossible	imposible	eem-po-**see**-ble
to improve	mejorar	me-kho-**rar**
in	dentro de; en	**dentro** de; en

English	Spanish	Pronunciation
in in two minutes	dentro de diez minutos	
in London	en Londres	
in front of	delante de	
included	incluido(a)	een-kloo-**ee**-do(a)
indigestion	la indigestión	een-dee-khes-**tyon**
indoors	dentro	
infection	la infección	een-fek-**thyon**
information	la información	een-for-ma-**thyon**
ingredients	los ingredientes	een-gre-**dyen**-tes
to injure	herir	e-**reer**
injured	herido(a)	e-**ree**-do(a)
inquiries	información	een-for-ma-**thyon**
insect	el insecto	een-**sek**-to
inside	dentro de	
instant coffee	el café instantáneo	ka-**fe** eens-tan-**ta**-ne-o
instead of	en lugar de	en loo**gar** de
insurance	el seguro	se-**goo**-ro
insurance	la póliza de	**po**-lee-tha de

English	Spanish	Pronunciation
certificate	seguros	se-**goo**-ros
to insure	asegurar	a-se-goo-**rar**
insured	asegurado(a)	a-se-goo-**ra**-do(a)
interesting	interesante	een-te-re-**san**-te
international	internacional	een-tair-na-thyo-**nal**
into	en	en
into town	al centro	
to introduce to	presentar a	pre-sen-**tar** a
invitation	la invitación	een-bee-ta-**thyon**
to invite	invitar	een-bee-**tar**
Ireland	Irlanda	eer-**lan**-da
Irish	irlandés/irlandesa	eer-lan-**des**/eer-lan-**de**-sa
iron (for clothes)	la plancha	**plancha**
to iron	planchar	planchar
island	la isla	**ees**la
it	lo/la	lo/la
to itch	picar	pee**kar**
it itches	pica	

English – Spanish

English	Spanish	Pronunciation
jacket	la chaqueta	cha-**ke**-ta
jam (food)	la mermelada	mair-me-**la**-da
January	enero	e-**ne**-ro
jar (honey, jam, etc)	el tarro	**ta**-rro
jeans	los vaqueros	ba-**ke**-ros
jeweller's	la joyería	kho-ye-**ree**-a
jewellery	las joyas	**kho**yas
job	el empleo	em-**ple**-o
to join (club, etc)	hacerse socio de	a-**thair**-se **so**-thyo de
to join in	participar en	par-tee-thee-**par** en
journey	el viaje	**bya**-khe
juice	el zumo	**thoo**mo
July	julio	**khoo**lyo
to jump	saltar	sal**tar**
June	junio	**khoo**nyo
just: *just two*	sólo dos	**so**-lo dos

K

English	Spanish	Pronunciation
to keep (to retain)	guardar	gwar**dar**
key	la llave	**lya**-be
card key (used in hotel)	la llave tarjeta	
to kill	matar	ma-**tar**
kilo(gram)	el kilo(gramo)	**kee**lo, kee-lo-**gra**-mo
kilometre	el kilómetro	kee-**lo**-me-tro
kind (person)	amable	a-**ma**-ble
kind (sort)	la clase	**kla**-se
what kind?	¿qué clase?	
to knock (door)	llamar	lya-**mar**
to know (have knowledge of) (person, place)	saber	sa-**bair**
	conocer	ko-no-**thair**

L

English	Spanish	Pronunciation
ladies (toilet)	los servicios de señoras	sair-**bee**-thyos de se-**nyo**-ras
lady	la señora	se-**nyo**-ra

English	Spanish	Pronunciation
lager	la cerveza (rubia)	thair-**be**-tha (**roob**ya)
lamp	la lámpara	**lam**-pa-ra
to land	aterizar	a-te-rree-**thar**
language	el idioma; la lengua	ee-**dyo**-ma; **len**gwa
large	grande	**gran**de
last	último(a)	**ool**-tee-mo(a)
late	tarde	**tar**de
later	más tarde	mas **tar**de
to laugh	reírse	re-**eer**-se
lavatory (house)	el wáter	el **wa**-tair
(in public place)	los servicios	los sair-**bee**-thyos
laxative	el laxante	lak-**san**-te
to learn	aprender	a-pren-**dair**
leather	el cuero	**kwe**-ro
to leave (a place)	irse de	**eer**se de
(leave behind)	dejar	de-**khar**
left:		
on/to the left	a la izquierda	a la eeth-**kyair**-da
left-luggage	la consigna	kon-**seeg**-na
leg	la pierna	la **pyair**na
lemon	el limón	**lee**mon
lemonade	la gaseosa	ga-se-**o**-sa
length	la longitud	lon-khee-**tood**
lens (photo)	el objetivo	ob-khe-**tee**-bo
(contact lens)	la lentilla	len-**tee**-lya
less	menos	**me**-nos
to let (to allow)	permitir	pair-mee-**teer**
(to hire out)	alquilar	al-kee-**lar**
letter	la carta	**kar**ta
(of alphabet)	la letra	**le**-tra
licence	el permiso	pair-**mee**-so
(driving)	el carné de conducir	karne de kon-doo-**theer**
to lie down	acostarse	a-kos-**tar**-se
lift (elevator)	el ascensor	as-then-**sor**
light (not heavy)	ligero(a)	lee-**khe**-ro(a)
light	la luz	luth
like (similar to)	como	**ko**-mo
line (row, queue)	la fila	**fee**la
(telephone)	la línea	**lee**-ne-a

English – Spanish

English – Spanish

English	Spanish	Pronunciation
list	la lista	**lees**ta
to listen to	escuchar	es-koo-**char**
litre	el litro	**lee**tro
little	pequeño(a)	pe-**ke**-nyo(a)
a little...	un poco de...	
to live	vivir	bee-**beer**
local	de la región; del país	de la re-**khyon**; del pa-**ees**
to lock	cerrar con llave	the-**rrar** kon **lya**-be
long	largo(a)	**lar**go(a)
to look after	cuidar	**kwee**dar
to look at	mirar	mee-**rar**
to look for	buscar	**boos**kar
to lose	perder	**pair**dair
lost	perdido(a)	pair-**dee**-do(a)
lost property office	la oficina de objetos perdidos	o-fee-**thee**-na de ob-**khe**-tos pair-**dee**-dos
lot: *a lot of*	mucho	**moo**cho
loud (sound, voice)	fuerte	**fwair**te
(volume)	alto(a)	**al**-to(a)
lounge	el salón	sa-**lon**
love	el amor	a-**mor**
to love (person)	querer	ke-**rair**
lovely	precioso(a)	pre-**thyo**-so(a)
low	bajo(a)	**ba**-jo(a)
low-fat	bajo(a) en calorías	**ba**-kho en ka-lo-**ree**-as
lucky: *to be lucky*	tener suerte	te-**nair** swairte
luggage	el equipaje	e-kee-**pa**-khe
luggage trolley	el carrito	ka-**rree**-to
lunch	la comida	ko-**mee**-da
M		
magazine	la revista	re-**bees**-ta
maid (in hotel)	la camarera	ka-ma-**re**-ra
mail	el correo	ko-**rre**-o
by mail	por correo	
main	principal	preen-thee-**pal**
main course (of meal)	el plato principal	**pla**-to preen-thee-**pal**
to make	hacer	a-**thair**

English	Spanish	Pronunciation
make-up	el maquillaje	ma-kee-**lya**-khe
male	masculino(a)	mas-koo-**lee**-no
man	el hombre	**ombre**
manager	el/la gerente	khe-**ren**-te
many	muchos(as)	**moochos**(as)
map (country)	el mapa	**ma**-pa
(of town)	el plano	**pla**-no
March	marzo	**mar**tho
marmalade	la mermelada de naranja	mair-me-**la**-da de na-**ran**-kha
married	casado(a)	ka-**sa**-do(a)
material (cloth)	la tela	**te**-la
to matter	importar	eem-por-**tar**
it doesn't matter	no importa	
May	mayo	**ma**-yo
meal	la comida	ko-**mee**-da
to mean	querer decir	ke-**rair** de-**theer**
to measure	medir	me-**deer**
meat	la carne	**karne**
medicine	la medicina	me-dee-**thee**-na

English	Spanish	Pronunciation
medium rare (meat)	medio(a)	**me**-dyo(a)
	hecho(a)	e-cho(a)
to meet (by chance)	encontrarse con	en-kon-**trar**-se kon
(by arrangement)	ver	bair
men	los hombres	**ombres**
menu	la carta	**karta**
message	el mensaje	men-**sa**-khe
metre	el metro	**me**-tro
metro (underground)	el metro	**me**-tro
metro station	la estación de metro	es-ta-**thyon** de **me**-tro
middle	el medio	**me**-dyo
midnight	la medianoche	me-dya-**no**-che
at midnight	a medianoche	
milk	la leche	**le**-che
fresh milk	la leche fresca	
hot milk	la leche caliente	
semi-skimmed milk	la leche semidesnatada	

English – Spanish

English	Spanish	Pronunciation
skimmed milk	la leche desnatada	
mineral water	el agua mineral	a-gwa-mee-ne-**ral**
minimum	el mínimo	**mee**-nee-mo
minute	el minuto	mee-**noo**-to
to miss (train, etc)	perder	pair-**dair**
Miss	la señorita	se-nyo-**ree**-ta
missing (lost)	perdido(a)	pair-**dee**-do(a)
my son is missing	se ha perdido mi hijo	
mistake	el error	e-**rror**
mobile (phone)	el teléfono móvil	te-**le**-fo-no **mo**-beel
mobile number	el número de móvil	noo-me-ro de **mo**-beel
modern	moderno(a)	mo-**dair**-no(a)
moment	el momento	mo-**men**-to
Monday	el lunes	**loo**-nes
money	el dinero	dee-**ne**-ro
month	el mes	mes
more	más	mas
morning	la mañana	ma-**nya**-na

English	Spanish	Pronunciation
mother	la madre	**ma**-dre
mother-in-law	la suegra	**swe**-gra
motor	el motor	mo-**tor**
motorbike	la moto	**mo**-to
motorway	la autopista	ow-to-**pees**-ta
mouth	la boca	**bo**-ka
to move	mover	mo-**bair**
movie	la película	pe-**lee**-koo-la
Mr	el señor (Sr.)	se-**nyor**
Mrs	la señora (Sra.)	se-**nyo**-ra
Ms	la señora (Sra.)	se-**nyo**-ra
much	mucho(a)	**moo**cho(a)
too much	demasiado(a)	
mugging	el atraco	a-**tra**-ko
muscle	el músculo	**moos**-koo-lo
museum	el museo	mu-**se**-o
music	la música	**moo**-see-ka
must (to have to)	deber	de-**bair**

N

name	el nombre	nombre
napkin	la servilleta	sair-bee-**lye**-ta
narrow	estrecho(a)	es-**tre**-cho(a)
national	nacional	na-thyo-**nal**
nationality	la nacionalidad	na-thyo-na-lee-**dad**
natural	natural	na-too-**ral**
nature	la naturaleza	na-too-ra-**le**-tha
near to	cerca de	**thair**ka de
necessary	necesario(a)	ne-the-**sa**-ryo
to need	necesitar	ne-the-see-**tar**
never	nunca	**noon**ka
new	nuevo(a)	**nwe**-bo(a)
news (TV, radio, etc)	las noticias	no-**tee**-thyas
newspaper	el periódico	pe-**ryo**-dee-ko
New Year	el Año Nuevo	a-nyo **nwe**-bo
New Zealand	Nueva Zelanda	**nwe**-bath-**lan**-da
next	próximo(a)	**prok**-see-mo(a)
nice (person)	simpático(a)	seem-**pa**-tee-ko(a)
(place, holiday)	bonito(a)	bo-**nee**-to(a)

niece	la sobrina	so-**bree**-na
night	la noche	**no**-che
no	no	no
nobody	nadie	**na**-dye
noise	el ruido	**rwee**do
none	ninguno(a)	neen-**goo**-no(a)
non-smoker	el/la no fumador(a)	no foo-ma-**dor**(a)
north	el norte	**norte**
Northern Ireland	Irlanda del Norte	eer-**lan**-da del **norte**
nose	la nariz	na-**reeth**
not	no	no
nothing	nada	**na**-da
notice (sign) (warning)	el anuncio	a-**noon**-thyo
	el aviso	a-**bee**-so
November	noviembre	no-**byem**-bre
now	ahora	a-**o**-ra
number	el número	**noo**-me-ro

English – Spanish

O

English	Spanish	Pronunciation
to obtain	obtener	ob-te-**nair**
October	octubre	ok-**too**-bre
of	de	de
off (light, etc)	apagado(a)	a-pa-**ga**-do(a)
(rotten)	pasado(a)	pa-**sa**-do(a)
office	la oficina	o-fee-**thee**-na
often	a menudo	a me-**noo**-do
how often?	¿cada cuánto?	
OK	¡vale!	¡**ba**-le!
old	viejo(a)	**bye**-kho(a)
on (light, TV, machine)	encendido(a)	en-then-**dee**-do(a)
once	una vez	**oo**na beth
at once	en seguida	
only	sólo	**so**-lo
open	abierto(a)	a-**byair**to(a)
to open	abrir	a-**breer**
opposite (to)	enfrente (de)	en-**fren**-te (de)
or	o	o
orange (fruit)	la naranja	na-**ran**-kha
(colour)	naranja	na-**ran**-kha
orange juice	el zumo de naranja	**thoo**mo de na-**ran**-kha
order: out of order	averiado(a)	a-be-**rya**-do(a)
to order (in restaurant)	pedir	pe-**deer**
other: the other one	el/la otro(a)	**o**-tro(a)
our	nuestro(a)	**nwes**tro(a)
out (light)	apagado(a)	a-pa-**ga**-do(a)
over (on top of)	(por) encima de	(por)en-**thee**-ma de
to be overbooked	tener overbooking	o-bair-**boo**-keeng
to overcharge	cobrar de más	ko-**brar** de mas
overdone (food)	demasiado(a) hecho(a)	de-ma-**sya**-do(a) e-**cho**(a)
to owe	deber	de-**bair**
owner	el/la propietario(a)	pro-pye-**ta**-rvo(a)

P

English	Spanish	Pronunciation
package tour	el viaje organizado	**bya**-khe or-ga-nee-**tha**-do
packet	el paquete	pa-**ke**-te
paid	pagado(a)	pa-**ga**-do(a)
pain	el dolor	do-**lor**
painful	doloroso(a)	do-lo-**ro**-so(a)
painting (picture)	el cuadro	**kwa**-dro
pair	el par	par
palace	el palacio	pa-**la**-thyo
pale	pálido(a)	**pa**-lee-do(a)
pants (men's underwear)	los calzoncillos	kal-thon-**thee**-lyos
paper	el papel	pa-**pel**
parcel	el paquete	pa-**ke**-te
pardon?	¿cómo?	¿**ko**-mo?
parents	los padres	**pa**-dres
park	el parque	**par**ke
to park	aparcar	a-par-**kar**
parking meter	el parquímetro	par-**kee**-me-tro
partner (business) (boy/girlfriend)	el/la socio(a) el/la compañero(a)	**so**-thyo(a) kom-pa-**nye**-ro(a)
party (group)	el grupo	**groo**po
party (celebration)	la fiesta	**fye**sta
passenger	el/la pasajero(a)	pa-sa-**khe**-ro(a)
passport	el pasaporte	pa-sa-**por**-te
pastry (dough)	la masa	**ma**-sa
(cake)	el pastel	pa**stel**
to pay	pagar	pa-**gar**
payment	el pago	**pa**-go
payphone	el teléfono público	te-**le**-fo-no **poo**-blee-ko
peach	el melocotón	me-lo-ko-**ton**
pear	la pera	**pe**-ra
peas	los guisantes	gee-**san**-tes
to peel (fruit)	pelar	pe-**lar**
pen	el bolígrafo; el boli	bo-**lee**-gra-fo; **bo**-lee
pensioner	el/la pensionista	pen-syo-**nees**-ta
people	la gente	**khen**te

English - Spanish

pepper (spice)	la pimienta	pee-**myen**-ta
pepper (vegetable)	el pimiento	pee-**myen**-to
per	por	por
per day	al día	
per hour	por hora	
per week	a la semana	
per person	por persona	
perhaps	quizá(s)	keetha(s)
person	la persona	pair-**so**-na
petrol	la gasolina	ga-so-**lee**-na
unleaded petrol	la gasolina sin plomo	
petrol station	la gasolinera	ga-so-lee-**ne**-ra
pharmacy	la farmacia	far-**ma**-thya
phone (mobile)	el teléfono	te-**le**-fo-no
	el móvil	**mo**-beel
by phone	por teléfono	
to phone	llamar por teléfono	lya-**mar** por te-**le**-fo-no
phonebook	la guía (telefónica)	**gee**-a (te-le-**fo**-nee-ka)

phonebox	la cabina (telefónica)	ka-**bee**-na (te-le-**fo**-nee-ka)
phone call	la llamada (telefónica)	lya-**ma**-da (te-le-**fo**-nee-ka)
phonecard	la tarjeta telefónica	tar-**khe**-ta te-le-**fo**-nee-ka
to photocopy	fotocopiar	fo-to-ko-**pyar**
photograph	la fotografía	fo-to-gra-**fee**-a
to take a photograph	hacer una fotografía	
piece	el trozo	**tro**-tho
pillow	la almohada	al-mo-**a**-da
pink	rosa	**ro**-sa
pity: what a pity!	¡qué pena!	ike pe-na!
place	el lugar	loo**gar**
place of birth	el lugar de nacimiento	loo**gar** de na-thee-**myen**-to
plan (of town)	el plano	**pla**-no
plane (airplane)	el avión	a-**byon**
plaster (sticking)	la tirita®	tee-**ree**-ta
(for broken limb)	la escayola	es-ka-**yo**-la

pepper – price list

plastic (made of)	de plástico	de plas-tee-ko
platform	el andén	an-den
play (theatre)	la obra	o-bra
to play (games)	jugar	khoogar
pleasant	agradable	a-gra-da-ble
please	por favor	por fa-bor
pleased	contento(a)	kon-ten-to(a)
p.m.	de la tarde	de la tarde
pocket	el bolsillo	bol-see-lyo
point	el punto	poonto
poisonous	venenoso(a)	ve-ne-no-so(a)
police (force)	la policía	po-lee-thee-a
police station	la comisaría	ko-mee-sa-ree-a
pool	la piscina	pees-thee-na
poor	pobre	po-bre
pork	el cerdo	thairdo
port (seaport)	el puerto	pwairto
(wine)	el oporto	o-por-to
porter (hotel)	el portero	por-te-ro
(at station)	el mozo	mo-tho
possible	posible	po-see-ble

post: *by post*	por correo	por ko-rre-o
to post	echar al correo	e-char al ko-rre-o
postbox	el buzón	boothon
postcard	la postal	postal
postcode	el código postal	ko-dee-go postal
post office	la oficina de Correos	o-fee-thee-na de ko-rre-os
potato	la patata	pa-ta-ta
pound (weight)	= approx. 0.5 kilo	
(money)	la libra	leebra
to prefer	preferir	pre-fe-reer
to prepare	preparar	pre-pa-rar
prescription	la receta médica	re-the-ta me-dee-ka
present (gift)	el regalo	re-ga-lo
pretty	bonito(a)	bo-nee-to(a)
price	el precio	pre-thyo
price list	la lista de precios	lees-ta de pre-thyos

English – Spanish

English – Spanish

English	Spanish	Pronunciation
private	privado(a)	pree-**ba**-do(a)
problem	el problema	pro-**ble**-ma
prohibited	prohibido(a)	pro-ee-**bee**-do(a)
to pronounce	pronunciar	pro-noon-**thyar**
how's it pronounced?	¿cómo se pronuncia?	
to provide	proporcionar	pro-por-thyo-**nar**
public holiday	la fiesta (oficial)	**fyes**ta (o-fee-**thyal**)
pudding	el postre	**postre**
to pull	tirar	tee**rar**
purse	el monedero	mo-ne-**de**-ro
to put (place)	poner	po-**nair**
pyjamas	el pijama	pee-**kha**-ma
Pyrenees	los Pirineos	pee-ree-**ne**-os
Q		
quality	la calidad	ka-lee-**dad**
quantity	la cantidad	kan-tee-**dad**
question	la pregunta	pre-**goon**-ta
queue	la cola	**ko**-la
to queue	hacer cola	a-**thair ko**-la
quick	rápido(a)	**ra**-pee-do(a)
quickly	de prisa	de **pree**sa
quiet (place)	tranquilo(a)	tran-**kee**-lo(a)
quite	bastante	bas-**tan**-te
quite expensive	bastante caro	
R		
race (sport)	la carrera	ka-**rre**-ra
racket (tennis, etc)	la raqueta	ra-**ke**-ta
radio	la radio	**ra**-dyo
railway	el ferrocarril	fe-rro-ka-**rreel**
rain	la lluvia	**lyoob**ya
to rain:		
it's raining	está lloviendo	esta lyo-**byen**-do
raincoat	el impermeable	eem-pair-me-**a**-ble
rape	la violación	byo-la-**thyon**
rare (unique)	excepcional	eks-thep-thyo-**nal**
(steak)	poco hecho(a)	**po**-ko **e**-cho(a)
rate (price)	la tarifa	ta-**ree**-fa

English	Spanish	Pronunciation
rate of exchange	el tipo de cambio	teepo de kambyo
raw	crudo(a)	kroodo(a)
razor	la maquinilla de afeitar	ma-kee-**nee**-lya de a-fey-**tar**
razor blades	las hojas de afeitar	o-khas de a-fey-**tar**
to read	leer	le-**air**
ready	listo(a)	**lees**to(a)
to get ready	prepararse	
real	verdadero(a)	bair-da-**de**-ro(a)
receipt	el recibo	re-**thee**-bo
reception desk	la recepción	re-thep-**thyon**
receptionist	el/la recepcionista	re-thep-thyo-**nees**-ta
to recommend	recomendar	re-ko-men-**dar**
red	rojo(a)	**ro**-kho(a)
to reduce	reducir	re-doo-**theer**
reduction	el descuento	des-**kwen**-to
refund	el reembolso	re-em-**bol**-so
to refuse	negarse	ne-**gar**-se

English	Spanish	Pronunciation
registered (letter)	certificado(a)	thair-tee-fee-**ka**-do(a)
registration form	la hoja de inscripción	o-kha de eens-kreep-**thyon**
to reimburse	reembolsar	re-em-bol-**sar**
relation (family)	el/la pariente	pa-**ryen**-te
relationship	la relación	re-la-**thyon**
I don't remember	acordarse (de) no me acuerdo	a-kor-**dar**-se (de)
to remove	quitar	keetar
to repair	la reparación	re-pa-ra-**thyon**
to repeat	reparar	re-pa-**rar**
to reply	repetir	re-pe-**teer**
to report	contestar	kon-tes-**tar**
reservation	informar	een-for-**mar**
to reserve	la reserva	re-**sair**-ba
reserved	reservar	re-sair-**bar**
rest (repose)	reservado(a)	re-sair-ba-**do**(a)
	el descanso	des-**kan**-so
(remainder)	el resto	**res**to

English – Spanish

198 | 199

English - Spanish

restaurant - seasoning		
to rest	descansar	des-kan-**sar**
restaurant	el restaurante	res-tow-**ran**-te
restaurant car	el coche restaurante	**ko**-che res-tow-**ran**-te
to return (to go back)	volver	bol**bair**
(to give back)	devolver	de-bol-**bair**
return (ticket)	de ida y vuelta	de **eeda** ee **bwel**ta
rice	el arroz	a-**rroth**
rich (person)	rico(a)	**reek**o(a)
(food)	pesado(a)	pe-**sa**-do(a)
right (correct)	correcto(a)	ko-**rrek**-to(a)
to be right	tener razón	te-**nair** ra-**thon**
right:		
on/to the right	a la derecha	a la de-**re**-cha
to ring (bell, to phone)	llamar	lya-**mar**
ring	el anillo	a-**nee**-lyo
road	la carretera	ka-rre-**te**-ra
road sign	la señal de tráfico	se-**nyal** de **tra**-fee-ko
roadworks	las obras	**o**-bras
roast	asado(a)	a-**sa**-do(a)
roll (bread)	el panecillo	pa-ne-**thee**-lyo
romantic	romántico(a)	ro-**man**-teek-o(a)
room (in house, hotel)	la habitación	a-bee-ta-**thyon**
(space)	sitio	**seet**yo
room number	el número de habitación	**noo**-me-ro de a-bee-ta-**thyon**
room service	el servicio de habitaciones	sair-**bee**-thyo de a-bee-ta-**thyo**-nes
rose	la rosa	**ro**-sa
rosé wine	el (vino) rosado	(**been**o) ro-**sa**-do
round (shape)	redondo(a)	re-**don**-do(a)
row (line, theatre)	la fila	**fee**la
to run	correr	ko-**rrair**

S

English	Spanish	Pronunciation
safe (secure)	seguro(a)	se-**goo**-ro(a)
(for valuables)	la caja fuerte	**ka**-kha **fwair**te
safety	la seguridad	se-goo-ree-**dad**
salad	la ensalada	en-sa-**la**-da
salami	el salchichón; el salami	sal-chee-**chon**; sa-**la**-mee
sale(s)	las rebajas	re-**ba**-khas
salesman/ woman	el/la vendedor(a)	ben-de-**dor**(a)
salt	la sal	sal
same	mismo(a)	**mees**mo(a)
sand	la arena	a-**re**-na
sandwich	el bocadillo; el sándwich	bo-ka-**dee**-lyo; **sang**weech
satellite dish	la antena parabólica	an-**te**-na pa-ra-**bo**-lee-ka
satellite TV	la televisión por satélite	te-le-bee-**syon** por sa-**te**-lee-te
Saturday	el sábado	**sa**-ba-do
sauce	la salsa	**sal**sa
to save (life)	salvar	sal**bar**
(money)	ahorrar	a-o-**rrar**
savoury	salado(a)	sa-**la**-do(a)
to say	decir	de-**theer**
scarf (woollen)	la bufanda	boo-**fan**-da
(headscarf)	el pañuelo	pa-nyoo-**e**-lo
school	la escuela	es-**kwe**-la
Scotland	Escocia	es-**ko**-thya
Scottish	escocés/ escocesa	es-ko-**thes**/ es-ko-**the**-sa
sea	el mar	mar
seafood	el/los marisco(s)	ma-**rees**-ko(s)
to search	buscar	boos**kar**
seasick	mareado(a)	ma-re-a-**do**(a)
seaside	la playa	**pla**-ya
at the seaside	en la playa	
season (of year)	la estación	es-ta-**thyon**
(holiday)	la temporada	tem-po-**ra**-da
seasonal	estacional	es-ta-thyo-**nal**
season ticket	el abono	a-**bo**-no
seasoning	el condimento	kon-dee-**men**-to

English - Spanish

English – Spanish

English	Spanish	Pronunciation
seat (chair)	la silla	**see**lya
(in bus, train)	el asiento	a-**syen**-to
seatbelt	el cinturón de seguridad	theen-too-**ron** de se-goo-ree-**dad**
second	segundo(a)	se-**goon**-do(a)
second (time)	el segundo	se-**goon**-do
second class	de segunda clase	de se-**goon**-da **kla**-se
to see	ver	bair
to sell	vender	ben**dair**
do you sell...?	¿tiene...?	
to send	enviar	en-bee-**ar**
September	septiembre	sep-**tyem**-bre
serious (accident, etc)	grave	**gra**-be
service (in church)	la misa	**mee**-sa
service (in restaurant)	el servicio	sair-**bee**-thyo
is service included?	¿está incluido el servicio?	

English	Spanish	Pronunciation
service charge	el servicio	sair-**bee**-thyo
service station	la estación de servicio	es-ta-**thyon** de sair-**bee**-thyo
serviette	la servilleta	sair-bee-**lye**-ta
set menu	el menú del día	me-**noo** del **dee**-a
several	varios(as)	**ba**-ryos(as)
sex	el sexo	**sek**so
shade	la sombra	**sombra**
shampoo	el champú	cham**poo**
to share	compartir; dividir	kom-par-**teer**; dee-bee-**deer**
to shave	afeitarse	a-fey-**tar**-se
shaver	la maquinilla de afeitar	ma-kee-**nee**-lya de a-fey-**tar**
sheet (bed)	la sábana	**sa**-ba-na
shirt	la camisa	ka-**mee**-sa
shoe	el zapato	tha-**pa**-to
shop	la tienda	**tyenda**
to shop	hacer compras; comprar	a-**thair kom**-pras; kom**prar**

English	Spanish	Pronunciation
shop assistant	el/la dependiente(a)	de-pen-**dyen**-te(a)
short	corto(a)	**kort**o(a)
shorts	los pantalones cortos	pan-ta-**lo**-nes **kort**os
shoulder	el hombro	**ombro**
to show	enseñar	en-se-**nyar**
shower (bath)	la ducha	**doo**cha
(rain)	el chubasco	choo-**bas**-ko
shut (closed)	cerrado(a)	the-**rra**-do(a)
sick (ill)	enfermo(a)	en-**fair**-mo(a)
sightseeing:		
to go sightseeing	hacer turismo	a-**thair** too-**rees**-mo
sign	la señal	se-**nyal**
to sign	firmar	feer**mar**
signature	la firma	**feerma**
silk	la seda	**se**-da
silver	la plata	**pla**-ta
similar to	parecido(a) a	pa-re-**thee**-do(a) a
since (time)	desde	**des**-de
(because)	puesto que	**pwes**to ke
since 1974	desde 1974	
to sing	cantar	kan**tar**
single (unmarried)	soltero(a)	sol-**te**-ro(a)
(bed, room)	individual	een-dee-bee-doo-**al**
sir	señor	sen**yor**
sister	la hermana	air-**ma**-na
to sit	sentarse	sen-**tar**-se
sit down, please	siéntese, por favor	
size (clothes)	la talla	**ta**-lya
(shoes)	el número	**noo**-me-ro
to ski	esquiar	es-kee-**ar**
ski boots	las botas de esquí	**bo**-tas de es**kee**
ski instructor	el/la monitor(a) de esquí	mo-nee-**tor**(a) de es**kee**
skin	la piel	pyel
skirt	la falda	**falda**

sky	el cielo	thye-lo	to snow	nevar	ne-**bar**
to sleep	dormir	dormeer	soap	el jabón	kha-**bon**
sleeping bag	el saco de dormir	**sa**-ko de dormeer	sober	sobrio(a)	**so**-bryo(a)
slice (of bread)	la rebanada	re-ba-**na**-da	sofa	el sofá	so-**fa**
(of ham)	la loncha	**lon**cha	soft	blando	**blando**
sliced bread	el pan de molde	pan de **molde**	soft drink	el refresco	re-**fres**-ko
slow	lento(a)	**len**to(a)	some	algunos(as)	al-**goo**-nos(as)
to slow down	reducir	re-doo-**theer**	someone	alguien	**algyen**
	la velocidad	la be-lo-thee-**dad**	something	algo	**algo**
slowly	despacio	des-**pa**-thyo	sometimes	a veces	a **be**-thes
small	pequeño(a)	pe-**ke**-nyo(a)	son	el hijo	**eekho**
smell	el olor	o-**lor**	soon	pronto	**pronto**
smile	la sonrisa	son-**ree**-sa	as soon as possible	lo antes posible	
to smile	sonreir	son-re-**eer**	sore throat	el dolor de	do-**lor** de
to smoke	fumar	foo**mar**		garganta	gar-**gan**-ta
smoke	el humo	**oomo**	sorry; sorry!	¡perdón!	¡pardon!
snack	el tentempié	ten-ten-**pye**	soup	la sopa	**so**-pa
to have a snack	tomar algo		south	el sur	soor
to sneeze	estornudar	es-tor-noo-**dar**	souvenir	el souvenir	soo-be-**neer**
snow	la nieve	**nye**-be	Spain	España	es-**pa**-nya
			Spanish	español(a)	es-pa-**nyol**(a)

English	Spanish	Pronunciation
sparkling	espumoso(a)	es-**poo**-mo-so(a)
to speak	hablar	a-**blar**
special	especial	es-pe-**thyal**
speciality	la especialidad	es-pe-thya-lee-**dad**
speed	la velocidad	be-lo-thee-**dad**
speeding	el exceso de velocidad	eks-**the**-so de be-lo-thee-**dad**
speed limit	la velocidad máxima	be-lo-thee-**dad mak**-see-ma
spell:		
how is it spelt?	¿cómo se escribe?	¿**ko**-mo se es-**kree**-be?
to spend *(money)*	gastar	gastar
spicy	picante	pee-**kan**-te
to spill	derramar	de-rra-**mar**
spirits	el alcohol	alkol
spoon	la cuchara	koo-**cha**-ra
sport	el deporte	de-**por**-te
sports centre	el polideportivo	po-lee-de-por-**tee**-bo
sports shop	la tienda de deportes	**tyen**da de-**por**-tes
spring *(season)*	la primavera	pree-ma-**be**-ra
(metal)	el muelle	**mwe**-lye
square *(in town)*	la plaza	**pla**-tha
to squeeze	apretar	a-pre-**tar**
(lemon)	exprimir	eks-pree-**meer**
stadium	el estadio	es-**ta**-dyo
stain	la mancha	**mancha**
stairs	las escaleras	es-ka-**le**-ras
stamp *(postage)*	el sello	**se**-lyo
to stand	estar de pie	estar de pye
star	la estrella	es-**tre**-lya
to start *(car)*	poner en marcha	po-**nair** en **marcha**
starter *(in meal)*	entrante	en-**tran**-te
station	la puesta en marcha	**pwes**ta en **marcha**
stay	la estación	es-ta-**thyon**
to stay *(remain)*	la estancia	es-**tan**-thya
	quedarse	ke-**dar**-se

English – Spanish

I'm staying at the hotel...	estoy alojado(a) en el hotel...		story	la historia	ees-**to**-rya
steak	el filete	fee-**le**-te	straightaway	inmediatamente	een-me-dya-ta-**men**-te
to steal	robar	ro-**bar**	straight on	todo recto	**to**-do **rek**to
steel	el acero	a-**the**-ro	strawberry	la fresa	**fre**-sa
is it steep?	¿hay mucha subida?	¿aee **moo**cha soo-**bee**-da?	street	la calle	**ka**-lye
step	el peldaño	pel-**da**-nyo	street map	el plano de la ciudad	**pla**-no de la thyoo**dad**
sterling (pounds)	las libras esterlinas	**lee**bras es-tair-**lee**-nas	strength	la fuerza	**fwair**tha
to stick (with glue)	pegar	pe-**gar**	stroke (medical)	la trombosis	trom-**bo**-sees
still (not fizzy)	sin gas	seen gas	strong	fuerte	**fwair**te
stomach	el estómago	es-**to**-ma-go	student	el/la estudiante	es-too-**dyan**-te
stomach upset	el trastorno estomacal	tras-**tor**-no es-to-ma-**kal**	stung	picado(a)	pee-**ka**-do(a)
stone	la piedra	**pye**-dra	suddenly	de repente	de re-**pen**-te
to stop	parar	pa-**rar**	suede	el ante	**an**te
store (shop)	la tienda	**tyen**da	sugar	el azúcar	a-**thoo**-kar
storm	la tormenta	tor-**men**-ta	sugar-free	sin azúcar	seen a-**thoo**-kar
(at sea)	el temporal	tem-po-**ral**	to suggest	sugerir	soo-khe-**reer**
			suit (men's and women's)	el traje	**tra**-khe
			suitcase	la maleta	ma-**le**-ta

English	Spanish	Pronunciation
summer	el verano	be-**ra**-no
sun	el sol	sol
to sunbathe	tomar el sol	to-**mar** el sol
sunblock	la protección solar	pro-tek-**thyon** so-**lar**
sunburn	la quemadura del sol	ke-ma-**doo**-ra del sol
suncream	el protector solar	pro-tek-**tor** so-**lar**
Sunday	el domingo	do-**meen**-go
sunglasses	las gafas de sol	**ga**-fas de sol
sunny:		
it's sunny	hace sol	**a**-the sol
sunscreen	el filtro solar	**feel**tro so-**lar**
sunstroke	la insolación	een-so-la-**thyon**
supermarket	el supermercado	soo-pair-mair-**ka**-do
supper	la cena	**the**-na
supplement	el suplemento	soo-ple-**men**-to
surname	el apellido	a-pe-**lyee**-do
surprise	la sorpresa	sor-**pre**-sa
to survive	sobrevivir	so-bre-bee-**beer**
to sweat	sudar	soo**dar**
sweet (not savoury)	dulce	**dool**the
sweet (dessert)	el dulce	**dool**the
sweetener	el edulcorante	e-dool-ko-**ran**-te
sweets	los caramelos	ka-ra-**me**-los
to swell (injury, etc)	hincharse	een-**char**-se
to swim	nadar	na-**dar**
swimming pool	la piscina	pees-**thee**-na
swimsuit	el bañador	ba-nya-**dor**
to switch off	apagar	a-pa-**gar**
to switch on	encender	en-then-**dair**
swollen	hinchado(a)	een-**cha**-do(a)
T		
table	la mesa	**me**-sa
tablet (pill)	la pastilla	pas-**tee**-lya
to take (medicine, etc)	tomar	to-**mar**

English – Spanish

English	Spanish	
how long does it take?	¿cuánto tiempo se tarda?	¿cwan-to tyem-po se tar-da?
to take off	despegar	des-pe-**gar**
to take out (of bag, etc)	sacar	sa-**kar**
to talk to	hablar con	a-**blar** kon
tall	alto(a)	**al**to(a)
taste	el sabor	el sa-**bor**
to taste	probar	pro-**bar**
can I taste it?	¿puedo probarlo?	¿pwe-do pro-bar-lo?
tax	el impuesto	eem-**pwes**-to
taxi	el taxi	tak-see
tea	el té	te
teeth	los dientes	dyentes
telephone	el teléfono	te-**le**-fo-no
to telephone	llamar por teléfono	lya-**mar** por te-**le**-fo-no
telephone box	la cabina (telefónica)	ka-**bee**-na (te-le-**fo**-nee-ka)
telephone call	la llamada (telefónica)	lya-**ma**-da (te-le-**fo**-nee-ka)

telephone card	la tarjeta telefónica
telephone directory	la guía (telefónica)
telephone number	el número de teléfono
television	la televisión
to tell	decir
temperature	la temperatura
to have a temperature	tener fiebre
temporary	provisional
tennis	el tenis
to test (try out)	probar
to thank	agradecer
thank you	gracias
that	ese/ésa/eso
that one	él/la/los/las
the	el/la/los/las
theatre	el teatro
theft	el robo

take off – tobacco

English	Spanish	pronunciation
there (over there)	allí	a-**lyee**
there is/	hay	aee
there are		
these	estos/estas	**estos/estas**
they	ellos/ellas	e-lyos/e-lyas
thick (not thin)	grueso(a)	**grwe**-so(a)
thief	el ladrón/	la-**dron**/
	la ladrona	la-**dro**-na
thin (person)	delgado(a)	del-**ga**-do(a)
thing	la cosa	**ko**-sa
my things	mis cosas	
to think	pensar	pensar
thirsty: I'm thirsty	tengo sed	tengo sed
this	este/esta/esto	**este/esta/esto**
this one	éste/ésta	**éste/ésta**
those	esos/esas	e-sos/e-sas
those ones	ésos/ésas	
throat	la garganta	gar-**gan**-ta
thunderstorm	la tormenta	tor-**men**-ta
Thursday	el jueves	khwe-bes
ticket (bus, etc)	el billete	bee-**lye**-te

English	Spanish	pronunciation
ticket office	el despacho de	des-**pa**-cho de
	billetes	bee-**lye**-tes
tidy	arreglado(a)	a-rre-**gla**-do(a)
to tidy up	ordenar	or-de-**nar**
tie	la corbata	kor-**ba**-ta
tight (fitting)	ajustado(a)	a-khoos-**ta**-do(a)
tights	las medias	**me**-dyas
till (cash desk)	la caja	**ka**-kha
(until)	hasta	**as**-ta
till 2 o'clock	hasta las 2	
time	el tiempo	**tyem**po
(clock)	la hora	**o**-ra
timetable	el horario	o-**ra**-ryo
tip	la propina	pro-**pee**-na
tired	cansado(a)	kan-**sa**-do(a)
tissues	los kleenex®	**klee**neks
to	a	a
to the airport	al aeropuerto	
toast (to eat)	la tostada	tos-**ta**-da
(raising glass)	el brindis	**breen**dees
tobacco	el tabaco	ta-**ba**-ko

English – Spanish

English - Spanish

tobacconist's	el estanco	el es-**tan**-ko
today	hoy	oy
together	juntos(as)	**khoon**tos(as)
toilet	los servicios; los aseos;	a-**se**-os;
toilet for disabled	los servicios para minusválidos	sair-**bee**-thyos
tomato	el tomate	to-**ma**-te
tomorrow	mañana	ma-**nya**-na
tongue	la lengua	**len**gwa
tonic water	la tónica	to-nee-ka
tonight	esta noche	esta **no**-che
too (also)	también	tam**byen**
tooth	el diente	**dyen**te
toothache	el dolor de muelas	do-**lor** de **mwe**-las
toothbrush	el cepillo de dientes	the-**pee**-lyo de **dyen**tes
toothpaste	la pasta de dientes	**pas**ta de **dyen**tes

top (of hill)	la cima	**thee**ma
(shirt)	el top	top
(t-shirt)	la camiseta	ka-mee-**se**-ta
on top of...	sobre...	
total (amount)	el total	to-**tal**
tour (trip)	el viaje	**bya**-khe
(of museum, etc)	la visita	bee-**see**-ta
guided tour	la visita con guía	
tourist	el/la turista	too-**rees**-ta
tourist office	la oficina de turismo	o-fee-**thee**-na de too-**rees**-mo
town	la ciudad	thyoo**dad**
town centre	el centro de la ciudad	**then**tro de la thyoo**dad**
town hall	el ayuntamiento	a-yoon-ta-**myen**-to
town plan	el plano de la ciudad	**pla**-no de la thyoo**dad**
toy	el juguete	khoo-**ge**-te
traditional	tradicional	tra-dee-thyo-**nal**
traffic	el tráfico	**tra**-fee-ko

English	Spanish	Pronunciation
traffic jam	el atasco	a-**tas**-ko
traffic lights	el semáforo	se-**ma**-fo-ro
traffic warden	el/la guardia de tráfico	**gwar**-dya de **tra**-fee-ko
trailer	el remolque	re-**mol**-ke
train	el tren	tren
by train	en tren	en tren
tram	el tranvía	tran-**bee**-a
to translate	traducir	tra-doo-**theer**
to travel	viajar	bya-**khar**
travel agent's	la agencia de viajes	a-**khen**-thya de **bya**-khes
trip	la excursión	eks-koor-**syon**
trolley	el carrito	ka-**rree**-to
trouble	el apuro	a-**poo**-ro
to be in trouble	estar en apuros	
trousers	los pantalones	pan-ta-**lo**-nes
true	verdadero(a)	bair-da-**de**-ro(a)
to try (attempt)	probar	pro-**bar**
to try on (clothes)	probarse	pro-**bar**-se
t-shirt	la camiseta	ka-mee-**se**-ta

English	Spanish	Pronunciation
Tuesday	el martes	**martes**
to turn	girar	geerar
to turn around	girar	geerar
to turn off (light, etc)	apagar	a-pa-**gar**
to turn on (light etc)	cerrar	the-**rrar**
	encender	en-then-**dair**
twice	abrir	a-**breer**
	dos veces	dos **be**-thes
typical	típico(a)	**tee**-pee-ko(a)

U

English	Spanish	Pronunciation
ugly	feo(a)	**fe**-o(a)
umbrella	el paraguas	pa-**ra**-gwas
(sunshade)	la sombrilla	som-**bree**-lya
uncle	el tío	**tee**-o
uncomfortable	incómodo(a)	een-**ko**-mo-do(a)
under	debajo de	de-**ba**-kho de
underground	el metro	**me**-tro
to understand	entender	en-ten-**dair**

English – Spanish

English – Spanish

I don't understand	no entiendo			
do you understand?	¿entiende?			
underwear	la ropa interior	ro-pa een-te-**ryor**	**vacant**	libre	**leebre**
United Kingdom	el Reino Unido	**rey**no oo-**nee**-do	**valid**	válido(a)	**ba**-lee-do(a)
United States	Estados Unidos	es-**ta**-dos oo-**nee**-dos	**valley**	el valle	**ba**-lye
			valuable	de valor	de ba-**lor**
unleaded petrol	la gasolina sin plomo	ga-so-**lee**-na seen **plo**-mo	**valuables**	los objetos de valor	ob-**khe**-tos de ba-**lor**
to unpack (suitcases)	deshacer las maletas	de-sa-**thair**-se las ma-**le**-tas	**value**	el valor	ba-**lor**
up: to get up	levantarse	le-ban-**tar**-se	**VAT**	el IVA	**eeba**
urgent	urgente	oor-**khen**-te	**vegetables**	las verduras	bair-**doo**-ras
to use	usar	oo**sar**	**vegetarian**	vegetariano(a)	be-khe-ta-**rya**-no(a)
useful	útil	**oo**teel	**very**	muy	mwee
			vest	la camiseta	ka-mee-**se**-ta
V			**vet**	el/la veterinario(a)	be-te-ree-**na**-ryo(a)
vacancy (in hotel)	la habitación libre	a-bee-ta-**thyon leeb**re	**via**	por	por
			view	la vista	**bees**ta
			village	el pueblo	**pwe**-blo
			vinegar	el vinagre	bee-**na**-gre
			virus	el virus	**bee**roos
			visa	el visado	bee-**sa**-do

English	Spanish	Pronunciation
visit	la visita	bee-**see**-ta
to visit	visitar	bee-see-**tar**
visitor	el/la visitante	bee-see-**tan**-te
voice	la voz	both
to vomit	vomitar	bo-mee-**tar**
voucher	el vale; el bono	**ba**-le; **bo**-no
W		
to wait for	esperar	es-pe-**rar**
waiter/waitress	el/la camarero(a)	ka-ma-**re**-ro(a)
waiting room	la sala de espera	**sa**-la-de es-**pe**-ra
Wales	Gales	**ga**-les
walk	un paseo	oon pa-**se**-o
to go for a walk	dar un paseo	
to walk	andar	an-**dar**
wallet	la cartera	kar-**te**-ra
to want	querer	ke-**rair**
I want	quiero	
warm	caliente	ka-**lyen**-te
it's warm (weather)	hace calor	

English	Spanish	Pronunciation
to warm up (milk, etc)	calentar	ka-len-**tar**
to wash (oneself)	lavar(se)	la-**bar**(se)
to watch (look at)	mirar	meerar
watch	el reloj	re-**lokh**
water	el agua	**a**-gwa
drinking water	el agua potable	
hot/cold water	el agua caliente/fría	
watermelon	la sandía	san-**dee**-a
way (manner)	la manera	ma-**ne**-ra
(route)	el camino	ka-**mee**-no
way in (entrance)	la entrada	en-**tra**-da
way out (exit)	la salida	sa-**lee**-da
weak (coffee, tea)	poco cargado(a)	**po**-ko kar-**ga**-do(a)
to wear	llevar	lye-**bar**
weather	el tiempo	**tyem**po
wedding	la boda	**bo**-da
Wednesday	el miércoles	**myair**-ko-les
week	la semana	se-**ma**-na

English – Spanish

English - Spanish

English	Spanish	Pronunciation
last week	la semana pasada	
next week	la semana que viene	
per week	por semana	
this week	esta semana	
weekend	el fin de semana	feen-de-se-**ma**-na
weekly	semanal	se-ma-**nal**
weight	el peso	**pe**-so
welcome!	¡bienvenido(a)!	¡byen-be-**nee**-do(a)!
well done (steak)	muy hecho(a)	mwee **e**-cho(a)
Welsh (language)	galés/galesa	ga-**les**/ga-**les**-a
west	el oeste	o-**es**-te
wet (weather)	mojado(a)	mo-**kha**-do(a)
lluvioso(a)	lyoo-**byo**-so(a)	
what?	¿qué?	¿ke?
when?	¿cuándo?	¿**kwan**do?
where?	¿dónde?	¿**don**de?
which?	¿cuál?	¿kwal?
which one?	¿cuál?	
which ones?	¿cuáles?	
while: *in a while*	dentro de un rato	
white	blanco(a)	
who?	¿quién?	
whole	entero(a)	
wholemeal bread	el pan integral	
whose?	¿de quién?	
why?	¿por qué?	
wide	ancho(a)	
wife	la mujer	
to win	ganar	
wind	el viento	
window (shop)	el escaparate	
(in car, train)	la ventanilla	
wine	el vino	
wine list	la carta de vinos	
winter	el invierno	
with	con	
with ice	con hielo	
dentro de oon ra-to		
blanko(a)		
¿kyen?		
en-**te**-ro(a)		
pan een-te-**gral**		
¿de kyen?		
¿por ke?		
ancho(a)		
moo**khair**		
ga-**nar**		
byento		
ben-**ta**-na		
es-ka-pa-**ra**-te		
ben-ta-**nee**-lya		
beeno		
karta de **bee**nos		
een-**byair**-no		
kon		

with milk	con leche	
with sugar	con azúcar	
without	sin	seen
without ice	sin hielo	
without milk	sin leche	
without sugar	sin azúcar	
woman	la mujer	moo-**khair**
word	la palabra	pa-**la**-bra
work	el trabajo	tra-**ba**-kho
to work (person)	trabajar	tra-ba-**khar**
(machine, car)	funcionar	foon-thyo-**nar**
world	el mundo	**moon**do
worried	preocupado(a)	pre-okoo-**pa**-do(a)
worse	peor	pe-**or**
to write	escribir	es-kree-**beer**
please write it down	escríbalo, por favor	
wrong:		
what's wrong	¿qué pasa?	¿ke **pa**-sa?

X		
X-ray	la radiografía	ra-dyo-gra-**fee**-a
to x-ray	hacer una radiografía	a-**thair** oona ra-dyo-gra-**fee**-a

Y		
year	el año	**a**nyo
this year	este año	
next year	el año que viene	
last year	el año pasado	
yellow	amarillo(a)	a-ma-**ree**-lyo(a)
Yellow Pages	las páginas amarillas	**pa**-khee-nas a-ma-**ree**-lyas
yes	sí	see
yesterday	ayer	a-**yair**
yoghurt	el yogur	yo-**goor**
young	joven	**kho**-ben

Z		
zone	la zona	**tho**-na
zoo	el zoo	**tho**-o

English – Spanish

Spanish – English

A

a	to; at
a la estación	to the station
a las 4	at 4 o'clock
abajo	below; downstairs
abierto(a)	open
abrigo *m*	coat
abril *m*	April
abrir	to open; to turn on *(tap)*
abuela *f*	grandmother
abuelo *m*	grandfather
acabar	to finish
acampar	to camp
acceso *m*	access
no access	
acceso prohibido	no access
acceso vías	to the platforms
accidente *m*	accident
aceite *m*	oil
aceite de oliva	olive oil
aceituna *f*	olive
aceptar	to accept
acompañar	to accompany
acuerdo *m*	agreement
¡de acuerdo!	OK; alright
alojamiento y desayuno	bed and breakfast
adelante	forward
adiós	goodbye; bye
admitir	to accept; to permit
no se admiten…	…not permitted
aduana *f*	customs
adulto(a) *m/f*	adult
aerolínea *f*	airline
aeropuerto *m*	airport
afeitarse	to shave
aficionado(a) *m/f*	fan *(cinema, jazz, etc)*
agencia *f*	agency
agencia inmobiliaria	estate agent's
agenda *f*	diary; personal organizer
agente de policía	policeman/ woman
agosto *m*	August
agradecer	to thank
agua *f*	water
agua caliente/ fría	hot/cold water
agua mineral	mineral water
ahora	now
ahorrar	to save *(money)*
ahumado(a)	smoked
aire *m*	air
aire acondicionado	air-conditioning
alarma *f*	alarm
albaricoque *m*	apricot
albergue *m*	hostel

Spanish – English

Spanish	English
alcanzar *m*	to reach; to get
alcohol *m*	alcohol; spirits
alcohólico(a)	alcoholic
alergia *f*	allergy
alérgico(a) a	allergic to something
algo	something
algodón *m*	cotton
alguien	someone
alguno(a)	some; any
algunos(as)	some; a few
alimentación *f*	grocer's; food
alimento *m*	food
allí	there (over there)
almacén *m*	store; warehouse
grandes almacenes	department stores
almendra *f*	almond
almohada *f*	pillow
almuerzo *m*	lunch
alojamiento *m*	accommodation
alquilar	to rent; to hire
se alquila	for hire
alquiler *m*	rent; rental
alquiler de coches	car hire
alrededor	about; around
alto(a)	high; tall
alta tensión	high voltage
altura *f*	altitude; height
amable	pleasant; kind
amarillo(a)	yellow; amber (traffic light)
ambulancia *f*	ambulance
ambulatorio *m*	health centre
América del Norte *f*	North America
amigo(a) *m/f*	friend
amor *m*	love
analgésico *m*	painkiller
análisis *m*	analysis
ancho *m*	width
anchoa *f*	anchovy (salted)
Andalucía *f*	Andalusia
andaluz(a)	Andalusian
andar	to walk
andén *m*	platform
angina (de pecho) *f*	angina
anillo *m*	ring
animal *m*	animal
aniversario *m*	anniversary
año *m*	year
Año Nuevo	New Year
ante *m*	suede
antes (de)	before
anticonceptivo *m*	contraceptive
antigüedades *f pl*	antiques
antiguo(a)	old; ancient
antihistamínico *m*	antihistamine

Spanish - English

Spanish	English
anular	to cancel
anunciar	to announce; to advertise
anuncio *m*	advertisement; notice
apagado(a)	off (light, etc)
apagar	to switch off; to turn off
aparato *m*	appliance
aparato de aire acondicionado	air-conditioning unit
aparcamiento *m*	car park
aparcar	to park
apartamento *m*	flat; apartment
apellido *m*	surname
apendicitis *f*	appendicitis
aperitivo *m*	aperitif (drink); appetizer; snack (food)
aprender	to learn
aquí	here
árbol *m*	tree
ardor de estómago *m*	heartburn
arena *f*	sand
armario *m*	wardrobe; cupboard
arreglar	to fix; to mend
arriba	upstairs; above
hacia arriba	upward(s)
arroz *m*	rice
arte *m*	art
artesanía *f*	crafts
articulación *f*	joint (body)
artículo *m*	article
artículos de regalo	gifts
asado(a)	roast
ascensor *m*	lift
asegurado(a)	insured
asegurar	to insure
aseos *mpl*	toilets
asiento *m*	seat
asistencia *f*	help; assistance
asistencia técnica	repairs
atacar	to attack
ataque *m*	fit (seizure)
ataque al corazón	heart attack
ataque de asma	asthma attack
atención *f*	attention
atención al cliente	customer service
aterrizar	to land
atraco *m*	mugging (person)
atrás	behind
atropellar	to knock down (car)
atún *m*	tuna fish
auténtico(a)	genuine; real
autobús *m*	bus

Spanish – English

autocar m — coach (bus)
autopista f — motorway
autor(a) mf — author
autoservicio m — self-service
Av. /Avda. — abbrev. for **avenida**
avena f — oats
avenida f — avenue
avería f — breakdown (car)
averiado(a) — out of order; broken down
avión m — airplane
aviso m — notice; warning
ayer — yesterday
ayudar — to help
ayuntamiento m — town/city hall
azafata f — air hostess; stewardess
azúcar m — sugar
azul — blue

B
bahía f — bay (along coast)
bailar — to dance
baile m — dance
bajar — to go down(stairs); to drop (temperature)
bajarse (del) — to get off (bus, etc)
bajo(a) — low; short; soft (sound)
balcón m — balcony
balón m — ball
bañador m — swimming costume/trunks
bañarse — to go swimming; to bathe; to have a bath
baño m — bath; bathroom
con baño — bathroom with bath

bar m — bar
barato(a) — cheap
barbacoa f — barbecue
barco m — ship; boat
barrio m — district; suburb
bastante — enough; quite
batido m — milkshake
to be — ser; estar
bebé m — baby
beber — to drink
bebida f — drink
bebida sin alcohol — soft drink
berenjena f — aubergine/ eggplant
besar — to kiss
beso m — kiss
biberón m — baby's bottle
bicicleta f — bicycle
bicicleta de montaña — mountain bike

Spanish – English

bien	well, good
bienvenido(a)	welcome
billete m	ticket
billete de ida	single ticket
billete de ida y vuelta	return ticket
bistec m	steak
blanco(a)	white
blando(a)	soft
blusa f	blouse
boca f	mouth
bocadillo m	sandwich (made with French bread)
boda f	wedding
bolígrafo m	biro; pen
bollo m	roll; bun
bolsa f	bag; Stock Exchange
bolsa de plástico	plastic bag
bolso m	handbag

bomberos mpl	fire brigade
bombilla f	light bulb
bombones mpl	chocolates
bonito(a)	pretty; nice-looking
bono m	voucher
bonobús m	bus pass
borracho(a)	drunk
bosque m	forest; wood
bota f	boot
bote m	boat; tin; can
bote salvavidas	lifeboat
botella f	bottle
botón m	button
bragas fpl	knickers
brazo m	arm
brillar	to shine
británico(a)	British
bronceado(a)	sun-tanned
bronceador m	suntan lotion
bucear	to dive

bueno(a)	good; fine
¡buenos días!	good morning!
¡buenas tardes!	good afternoon/ evening!
¡buenas noches!	good evening/ night!
bufanda f	scarf (woollen)
buscar	to look for
butacas tfpl	stalls (theatre)
buzón m	postbox; letterbox
buzón de voz	voicemail

C

caballeros mpl	gents
caballo m	horse
montar a caballo	to go riding
cabello m	hair
cabeza f	head
cabina f	cabin

cabina (telefónica) — phone box
cable *m* — wire; cable
cacahuete *m* — peanut
cacao *m* — cocoa
cada — every; each
cada día — daily (each day)
cada uno — each (one)
cadena — chain; channel (TV); WC chain (for cistern)
caducado(a) — out-of-date
café *m* — café; coffee
cafetería *f* — snack bar; café
caja *f* — cashdesk; box
caja de cambios — gearbox
caja fuerte — safe
cajero automático — cash dispenser; ATM
calamares *mpl* — squid
calambre *m* — cramp

caldo *m* — stock; consommé
calefacción *f* — heating
calentar — to heat up (milk, etc)
calidad *f* — quality
caliente — hot
calle *f* — street; fairway (golf)
calmante *m* — painkiller
calzado *m* — footwear
calzoncillos *mpl* — underpants
cama *f* — bed
camarera *f* — waitress; chambermaid
camarero *m* — barman; waiter
cambiar — to change; to exchange
cambiarse — to get changed

cambio *m* — change; exchange; gear (car)
caminar — to walk
camino *m* — path; road; route
camión *m* — lorry
camisa *f* — shirt
camiseta *f* — t-shirt; vest
camisón *m* — nightdress
camping *m* — campsite
campo *m* — countryside; field; pitch
campo de fútbol — football pitch
campo de golf — golf course
caña *f* — cane; rod
caña (de cerveza) — glass of beer
caña de pescar — fishing rod
Canadá *m* — Canada
canadiense — Canadian
cancelación *f* — cancellation

Spanish – English

cancelar	to cancel
cansado(a)	tired
cantidad f	quantity
capilla f	chapel
cara f	face
caramelo m	sweet; caramel
caravana f	caravan
carburante m	fuel
carga f	charge
cargador m	recharger
cargar	to load; charge to
cargar en	to charge to
cuenta	account
cargo m	charge
a cargo del	at the customer's
cliente	expense
carne f	meat
carné de	driving licence
conducir m	

carné de	identity card
identidad	
(DNI) m	
carnicería f	butcher's
caro(a)	dear; expensive
carretera f	road
carretera	secondary road,
comarcal	B-road
carretera	A-road
nacional	
carretera de	ring road
circunvalación	
carril m	lane (on road)
carta f	letter; playing
	card; menu
carta certificada f	registered letter
cartera f	wallet; briefcase
casa f	house; home;
	household
casado(a)	married
casco m	helmet

casi	almost
caso: en caso de	in case of
castañuelas ffpl	castanets
castellano(a)	Spanish;
	Castilian
castillo m	castle
católico(a)	Catholic
cava m	cava; sparkling
	white wine
ceder	to give way
ceda el paso	give way
celo m	Sellotape®
cementerio m	cemetery
cena f	dinner; supper
cenar	to have dinner
cenicero m	ashtray
centímetro m	centimetre
céntimo m	euro cent
centro m	centre
centro de	business centre
negocios	

Spanish	English
cepillo *m*	brush
cepillo de dientes	toothbrush
cerámica *f*	ceramics; pottery
cerca (de)	near; close to
cercanías *tfpl* tren de cercanías	suburban train
cerdo *m*	pig; pork
cereza *f*	cherry
cerillas *tfpl*	matches
cerrado(a)	closed
cerrado por reforma	closed for repairs
cerradura *f*	lock
certificado *m*	certificate
certificado(a)	registered
cervecería *f*	pub
cerveza *f*	beer; lager
chalet (*sing*); **chalets** (*pl*) *m*	villa
chaleco *m*	waistcoat
chaleco salvavidas	life jacket
champiñón *m*	mushroom
champú *m*	shampoo
chaqueta *f*	jacket
charcutería *f*	delicatessen
cheque *m*	cheque
cheque de viaje	traveller's cheque
chica *f*	girl
chico *m*	boy
chico(a)	small
chocar	to crash (*car*)
chocolate *m*	chocolate; hot chocolate
chorizo *m*	hard pork sausage
chuleta *f*	cutlet; chop
ciclista *mf*	cyclist
ciego(a)	blind
cigarrillo *m*	cigarette
cigarro *m*	cigar; cigarette
cine *m*	cinema
cinturón *m*	belt
cinturón de seguridad	safety belt
circulación *f*	traffic
circule por la derecha	keep right (*road sign*)
cita *f*	appointment
ciudad *f*	city; town
claro(a)	light (*colour*); clear
clase *f*	class; type; lesson
clase preferente	club/business class
clase turista	economy class
cliente *mf*	customer; client

Spanish – English

Spanish – English

Spanish	English
climatizado(a)	air-conditioned
clínica f	clinic; private hospital
cobrar	to charge; to cash
coche m	car; coach (on train)
cocina f	kitchen; cooker; cuisine
cocinar	to cook
coco m	coconut
codo m	elbow
coger	to catch; to get; to pick up (phone)
cola f	glue; queue; tail
colchón m	mattress
colegio m	school
colisionar	to crash
collar m	necklace
color m	colour
comedor m	dining room
comenzar	to begin
comer	to eat
comestibles mpl	groceries
comida f	food; meal
se sirven comidas	meals served
comidas caseras	home cooking
comisaría f	police station
como	as; like; since
¿cómo?	how?; pardon?
cómodo(a)	comfortable
completo(a)	full; no vacancies
compras	shopping
comprar	to buy
comprender	to understand
con	with
condón m	condom
conducir	to drive
conductor(a) m/f	driver
confirmación f	confirmation
confirmar	to confirm
congelado(a)	frozen
congelador m	freezer
conocer	to know; to be acquainted with
consumir	to eat; to use
consumir (preferente-mente) antes de...	best before...
contacto m	contact; ignition (car)
contagioso(a)	infectious
contaminado(a)	polluted
contento(a)	pleased
contestar	to answer; to reply
contra	against
contrato m	contract
control m	inspection; check

control de seguridad	security check	
copa f	glass; goblet	
copa de helado	mixed ice cream	
cordero m	lamb; mutton	
correcto(a)	right (correct)	
correo m	mail	
correo electrónico	e-mail	
Correos m	post office	
correr	to run	
corrida de toros f	bullfight	
corriente f	power; current (electric, water); draught (of air)	
cortado m	espresso coffee with dash of milk	
cortar	to cut	
corte m	cut	

corto(a)	short	
cosa f	thing	
costa f	coast	
costar	to cost	
crédito m	credit	
creer	to think; to believe	
crema f	cream (lotion)	
crema bronceadora/solar	suntan lotion	
crema de afeitar	shaving cream	
cruce m	junction; crossroads	
crudo(a)	raw	
cruzar	to cross	
cuadro m	picture; painting	
a/de cuadros	checked (pattern)	
¿cuál?	which?	
¿cuándo?	when?	
¿cuánto?	how much?	
¿cuántos?	how many?	

cuarto m	room	
cuarto de baño	bathroom	
cuarto de estar	living room	
cubrir	to cover	
cuchara f	spoon	
cucharilla f	teaspoon	
cuchillo m	knife	
cuenta f	bill; account	
cuero m	leather	
cuidado m	care	
¡cuidado!	look out!	
¡ten cuidado!	be careful!	
cumpleaños m	birthday	
curvas peligrosas f/pl	dangerous bends	

D

dar	to give	
dar marcha atrás	to reverse	
dar propina	to tip (waiter, etc)	

Spanish – English

Spanish – English

datos *mpl*	data; information	dentro (de)	inside
dcha.	*abbrev. for* **derecha**	dependiente(a) *mf*	sales assistant
de	of; from	deporte *m*	sport
de acuerdo	all right (agreed)	depósito de gasolina *f*	petrol tank
debajo (de)	under(neath)	derecha *f*	right(-hand side)
deber	to owe; to have to	*a la derecha*	on/to the right
decir	to tell; to say	derecho *m*	right; law
declarar	to declare	*derechos de aduana*	customs duty
dedo *m*	finger	derecho(a)	right; straight
dejar	to let; to leave	desayuno *m*	breakfast
dejar libre la salida	keep clear	descafeinado(a)	decaffeinated
delante de	in front of	descansar	to rest
delito *m*	crime	descanso *m*	rest; interval
demasiado	too much	descongelar	to defrost; to de-ice
demasiado	overdone	descuento *m*	discount; reduction
hecho(a)			
dentífrico *m*	toothpaste		
desde	since; from		
desenchufado(a)	off; disconnected; unplugged		
deshacer	to undo; to unpack		
desinfectante *m*	disinfectant		
desmaquilladora	make-up remover		
desnatado(a)	skimmed		
desodorante *m*	deodorant		
despacio	slowly; quietly		
despegar	to take-off; to remove; to peel off		
despertador *m*	alarm (clock)		
después	after; afterward(s)		
destino *m*	destination		
desvío *m*	detour; diversion		

Spanish	English
detalle m	detail; nice gesture
al detalle	retail
detener	to arrest
detrás (de)	behind
día m	day
día festivo/de fiesta	public holiday; holiday
día laborable/hábil	working day; weekday
diabético(a) mf	diabetic
diario(a)	daily
a diario	every day
diarrea f	diarrhoea
diciembre m	December
diente m	tooth
dieta f	diet
difícil	difficult
dificultad f	difficulty
dinero m	money
dinero (en) efectivo	cash
dirección f	direction; address; (Aut) steering; steering wheel; e-mail address
dirección de correo electrónico	e-mail address
dirección prohibida	no entry
dirección única	one-way
directo(a)	direct (train, etc)
disponible	available
distancia f	distance
distinto(a)	different
diversión f	fun
divertido(a)	funny (amusing)
divertirse	to enjoy oneself
divisa f	foreign currency
divorciado(a)	divorced
docena f	dozen
documentos mpl	documents
dolor m	ache; pain
dolor de cabeza	headache
dolor de garganta	sore throat
dolor de muelas	toothache
dolor de oídos	earache
domicilio m	home address
domingo m	Sunday
¿dónde?	where?
dormir	to sleep
dormitorio m	bedroom
dosis f	dose; dosage
droga f	drug
ducha f	shower
ducharse	to take a shower
dueño(a) mf	owner
durante	during

Spanish – English

Spanish – English

E

ecológico(a)	organic; environmentally friendly
edad *f*	age (of person)
edad mínima	age limit
EE.UU.	USA
el	the
él	he; him
electricidad *f*	electricity
electricista *mf*	electrician
elegir	to choose
ella	she; her
ello	it
ellos(as)	they; them
embajada *f*	embassy
embarazada	pregnant
embarque *m*	boarding
empezar	to begin
empleo *m*	employment; use

empresa *f*	firm; company
empujar	to push
empuje	push
en	in; into; on
encender	to switch on; to light
encender las luces	to switch on headlights
enchufe *m*	plug; point; socket
encima de	onto; on top of
encontrar	to find
encontrarse con	to meet
enero *m*	January
(by chance)	
enfadado(a)	angry
enfermedad *f*	disease
enfermera(o) *mf*	nurse
enfermo(a)	ill

enfrente (de)	opposite
ensalada *f*	salad
enseñar	to show; to teach
entender	to understand
entero(a)	whole
entrada *f*	entrance; admission; ticket
entrada principal	main entrance
entradas limitadas	limited tickets
entradas numeradas	numbered tickets
no hay entradas	sold out
entrada libre	admission free
entrar	to go in; to get in; to enter
entre	among; between
entremeses *mpl*	hors d'œuvres

enviar	to send	**escrito:**	in writing
envío m	shipment	**por escrito**	
envolver	to wrap	**escuchar**	to listen to
epiléptico(a) m	epileptic	**escultura** f	sculpture
equipaje m	luggage; baggage	**ese/esa**	that
		esos/esas	those
equipaje de mano	hand-luggage	**espacio** m	space
		espalda f	back (of body)
error m	mistake	**España** f	Spain
es	he/she/it is	**español(a)**	Spanish
escalera f	stairs; ladder	**especialidad** f	speciality
escalera de incendios	fire escape	**espectáculo** m	entertainment; show
escaparate m	shop window	**espejo** m	mirror
escoba f	broom (brush)	**espejo retrovisor**	rear-view mirror
escocés(cesa)	Scottish	**esperar**	to wait (for); to hope
Escocia f	Scotland	**esposa** f	wife
escoger	to choose	**esposo** m	husband
esconder	to hide	**esquí** m	skiing; ski
escribir	to write		

esquí acuático	water-skiing		
esquí de fondo	cross-country skiing		
esquiar	to ski		
esquina f	street corner		
está	you (formal)/ he/she/it is		
estación f	railway station; season		
estación de autobuses	bus/coach station		
estación de servicio	petrol/service station		
estadio m	stadium		
Estados Unidos mpl	United States		
estanco m	tobacconist's		
estar	to be		
este m	east		
éste/esta	this		
estómago m	stomach		

Spanish – English

Spanish – English

Spanish	English	Spanish	English	Spanish	English
estos/estas	these	factura f	receipt; bill; account	feo(a)	ugly
estrecho(a)	narrow	facturación f	check-in	feria f	trade fair; unfair
estrella f	star	falda f	skirt	ferrocarril m	railway
estropeado(a)	out of order; broken; damaged	falso(a)	fake; false	festivos mpl	public holidays
		farmacia f	chemist's; pharmacy	fiebre f	fever
euro m	euro	farmacia de guardia	duty chemist	fiesta f	party; public holiday
Europa f	Europe				
evitar	to avoid	faro m	headlamp; lighthouse	fila f	row; line (queue)
excursión f	tour; excursion	faro antiniebla	fog-lamp	filete m	fillet; steak
éxito m	success	favor m	favour	fin m	end
explicar	to explain	por favor	please	fin de semana	weekend
exportar	to export	favorito(a)	favourite	firma f	signature
exposición f	exhibition	febrero m	February	firmar	to sign
extintor m	fire extinguisher	fecha f	date	firme aquí	sign here
extranjero(a) mf	foreigner	fecha de caducidad	expiry date	floristería f	florist's shop
				fontanero m	plumber
F				foto f	picture; photo
fábrica f	factory	feliz	happy	fotocopia f	photocopy
fácil	easy	femenino(a)	feminine	fotografía f	photograph
				frágil	fragile
				francés(cesa)	French

Spanish	English
Francia f	France
frecuente	frequent
freir	to fry
frenar	to brake
freno m	brake
frente a	opposite
fresa f	strawberry
fresco(a)	fresh; crisp; cool
frío(a)	cold
frito(a)	fried
fruta f	fruit
fruta del tiempo	fruit in season
frutería f	fruit shop
fuera	outdoors; out
fuerte	strong; loud
fumadores mpl	smokers
fumar	to smoke
prohibido fumar	no smoking
función f	show
funcionar	to work; to function
no funciona	out of order

G

Spanish	English
gafas fpl	glasses
gafas de sol	sunglasses
galería f	gallery
galería de arte	art gallery
galés(lesa)	Welsh
Gales m	Wales
gallego(a)	Galician
galleta f	biscuit
ganar	to earn; to win (sports, etc)
garantía f	guarantee
garganta f	throat
gas m	gas
con gas	fizzy, sparkling
sin gas	non-fizzy; still
gaseosa f	lemonade
gasoil m	diesel
gasolina f	petrol
gasolina sin plomo	unleaded petrol
gasolinera f	petrol station
gastar	to spend (money)
gastos mpl	expenses
gato m	cat; jack (for car)
gente f	people
girar	to turn around
glorieta f	roundabout
goma f	rubber; eraser
gordo(a)	fat
gótico(a)	Gothic
gracias	thank you
muchas gracias	thank you very much
gramo m	gram(me)
Gran Bretaña f	Great Britain
grande	large; big; tall

Spanish - English

Spanish – English

grandes almacenes *mpl*	department store
gratis	free (costing nothing)
grave	serious (accident, etc)
gripe *f*	flu
gris	grey
grupo *m*	group; band (rock)
grupo sanguíneo	blood group
guantes *mpl*	gloves
guapo(a)	handsome; attractive
guardar	to put away; to keep
guardia *f*	guard
Guardia Civil	Civil Guard
guía (telefónica) *f*	phone directory
guiar	to guide

guitarra *f*	guitar
gustar	to like; to enjoy

H

habitación *f*	room
habitación doble	double room
habitación individual	single room
hablar (con)	to speak/talk to
se habla inglés	English spoken
hacer	to do; to make
hacer cola	to queue
hacer turismo	to sightsee
hacia	toward(s)
hacia arriba	upwards, up
hacia abajo	downwards, down
hacia adelante	forwards
hacia atrás	backwards
harina *f*	flour

hasta	until; till
hay	there is/ there are
hecho(a)	finished; done
hecho a mano	handmade
heladería *f*	ice-cream parlour
helado *m*	ice cream
hemorragia *f*	haemorrhage
herida *f*	wound; injury
hermano(a) *mf*	brother/sister
hervido(a)	boiled
hervir	to boil
hielo *m*	ice
con/sin hielo	with/without ice
hígado *m*	liver
hijo(a) *mf*	son/daughter
hinchado(a)	swollen
hipermercado *m*	hypermarket
histórico(a)	historic
hola	hello; hi!

hombre m	man
hombro m	shoulder
hora f	hour; appointment; time
horario m	timetable
horchata (de chufa) f	refreshing tiger nut drink
horno m	oven
al horno	baked; roasted
hospital m	hospital
hostal m	small hotel; hostel
hotel m	hotel
hoy	today
huelga f	strike (of workers)
hueso m	bone
huésped mf	guest
huevo m	egg
humo m	smoke

I

ida f	outward journey
de ida y vuelta	return (ticket)
idioma m	language
iglesia f	church
importar	to matter; to import (goods)
importe total m	total (amount)
imprescindible	essential
impreso m	form
impuesto m	tax
incluido(a)	included
inconsciente	unconscious
individual	individual; single
infarto m	heart attack
infección f	infection
inferior	inferior; lower
inflamación f	inflammation

informe m	report (medical, police)
infracción f	offence
infracción de tráfico	traffic offence
Inglaterra f	England
inglés(lesa)	English
insecto m	insect
insolación f	sunstroke
instrucciones f/pl	directions; instructions
interesante	interesting
interior	inside
intermitente m	indicator (in car)
interruptor m	switch
invierno m	winter
invitación f	invitation
invitado(a) mf	guest
invitar	to invite
inyección f	injection
ir	to go

Spanish – English

Spanish – English

ir a buscar	to fetch	*jamón (de) York*	cooked ham
irse a casa	to go home	*jardín m*	garden
irse de	to leave *(a place)*	*jefe(a) mf*	chief; head; boss
Irlanda f	Ireland	*joven*	young
Irlanda del	Northern	*joya f*	jewel
Norte f	Ireland	*joyas*	jewellery
irlandés(desa)	Irish	*joyería f*	jeweller's
isla f	island	*judías tfpl*	beans
Italia f	Italy	*judías verdes*	green beans
italiano(a)	Italian	*jueves m*	Thursday
itinerario m	route; schedule	*jugar*	to play; gamble
IVA m	VAT	*julio m*	July
izq./izqda.	abbrev. for	*juguete m*	toy
	izquierda	*juguetería f*	toy shop
izquierda f	left	*junio m*	June
		junto a	together
		junto a	next to
		juventud f	youth
J			
jabón m	soap	**K**	
jamás	never	*kilo m*	kilo(gram)
jamón m	ham		
jamón serrano	cured ham		

kilometraje m	mileage		
kilometraje	(un)limited		
(i)limitado	mileage		
kilómetro m	kilometre		
kiosko (de	newsstand		
prensa) m			
kleenex® m	tissue		
L			
la	the; her; it;		
	you *(formal)*		
labio m	lip		
laborable	working *(day)*		
laborables	weekdays		
lado m	side		
al lado de	beside		
ladrón(ona) mf	thief		
lago m	lake		
lámpara f	lamp		
lana f	wool		
lápiz m	pencil		

Spanish	English
largo(a)	long
largo recorrido	long-distance (train, etc)
lata f	can (container); tin
lavabo m	lavatory; washbasin
lavado(a)	washed
lavadora f	washing machine
lavar	to wash
lavarse	to wash oneself
leche f	milk
leche desnatada	skimmed milk
leche entera	wholemilk
leche semi-desnatada	semi-skimmed milk
lechuga f	lettuce
leer	to read
lejos	far
lengua f	language; tongue
lente f	lens
lentes de contacto	contact lenses
lentejas fpl	lentils
lentillas fpl	contact lenses
lento(a)	slow
letra f	letter (of alphabet)
levantar	to lift
levantarse	to get up; to rise
ley f	law
libra f	pound (currency, weight)
libra esterlina	pound sterling
libre	free/vacant
libre de impuestos	tax-free
librería f	bookshop
libro m	book
licencia f	permit; licence
licor m	liqueur
licores m	spirits
límite m	limit; boundary
límite de velocidad	speed limit
limón m	lemon
limonada f	lemonade
limpiar	to clean
limpieza en seco f	dry-cleaning
limpio(a)	clean
linterna f	torch; flashlight
liso(a)	plain; smooth
listo(a)	ready
litro m	litre
llamada f	call
llamar	to call; to ring; to knock (on door)
llave f	key; tap; spanner
llaves del coche	car keys

Spanish – English

Spanish – English

llegada f	arrival
llegar	to arrive; to come
llenar	to fill; to fill in
lleno(a)	full (up)
llevar	to bring; to wear; to carry
lluvia f	rain
local m	premises; bar
lugar m	place
lugar de nacimiento	place of birth
lujo m	luxury
luna f	moon
luna de miel	honeymoon
lunes m	Monday
luz f	light

M

macedonia f	fruit salad
madera f	wood
madre f	mother
maduro(a)	ripe; mature
mal/malo(a)	bad (weather, news)
maleta f	case; suitcase
maletero m	boot (car)
mañana f	tomorrow
mañana f	morning
mancha f	stain; mark
mando a distancia m	remote control
manera f	way; manner
mano f	hand
de segunda mano	secondhand
maquinilla de afeitar	shaver
manta f	blanket
mantener	to maintain; to keep
mantequilla f	butter

manzana f	apple; block (of houses)
manzanilla f	camomile tea; dry sherry
mapa m	map
mapa de carreteras	road map
maquillaje m	make-up
máquina f	machine
máquina de afeitar	razor
máquina de fotos	camera
mar m	sea
marcapasos m	pacemaker
marcha f	gear
marcha atrás	reverse gear
marea f	tide
marea alta/baja	high/low tide
mareado(a)	sick (car, sea); dizzy

Spanish	English
margarina *f*	margarine
marido *m*	husband
marisco *m*	seafood; shellfish
marisquería *f*	seafood restaurant
mármol *m*	marble
marrón	brown
marroquinería *f*	leather goods
martes *m*	Tuesday
marzo *m*	March
más	more; plus
más que	more than
más tarde	later
masculino(a)	male
matar	to kill
matrícula *f*	number plate
matrimonio *m*	marriage
mayo *m*	May
mayor	bigger; biggest
mayor de edad	adult

Spanish	English
mayores de 18 años	over-18s
mechero *m*	lighter
medianoche *f*	midnight
medias *f/pl*	tights; stockings
medicina *f*	medicine; drug
médico(a) *m/f*	doctor
medida *f*	measurement; size
medio *m*	the middle
medio(a)	half
media hora	half an hour
media pensión *f*	half board
mediodía:	midday; noon
Mediterráneo *m*	Mediterranean
mejor	best; better
mejor que	better than
melocotón *m*	peach
melón *m*	melon

Spanish	English
menor	smaller/ smallest; least
menos	minus; less; except
menos que	less than
mensaje *m*	message
mensual	monthly
menú *m*	menu
menú del día	set menu
mercado *m*	market
mercadillo	flea market
mermelada *f*	jam
mes *m*	month
mesa *f*	table
metro *m*	metre; underground; tape measure
mi	my
mí	me
miel *f*	honey
mientras	while

Spanish – English

Spanish – English

Spanish	English
miércoles m	Wednesday
mil	thousand
milímetro m	millimetre
minusválido(a) mf	disabled person
mirar	to look at; to watch
misa f	mass (in church)
mismo(a)	same
mitad f	half
mochila f	backpack; rucksack
moda f	fashion
modo m	way; manner
modo de empleo	instructions for use
mojado(a)	wet
moneda f	currency; coin
introduzca monedas	insert coins
monitor(a) de esquí mf	ski instructor
montaña f	mountain
montañismo m	mountaineering
montar	to ride
montar a caballo	to horse ride
mordedura f	bite
morder	to bite
mostrador m	counter; desk
mostrar	to show
moto(cicleta) f	(motor)bike
moto acuática	jet ski
móvil m	mobile phone
media pensión (MP)	half board
mucho	a lot; much
mucho(a)	a lot (of); much
muchos(as)	many
muela f	tooth
muestra f	exhibition; sample
mujer f	woman; wife
multa f	fine (to be paid)
mundo m	world
muñeca f	wrist; doll
museo m	museum; art gallery
muy	very
muy hecho(a)	well done (steak)

N

Spanish	English
nacional	national; domestic (flight)
nacionalidad f	nationality
nada	nothing
de nada	don't mention it
nada más	nothing else
nadar	to swim
nadie	nobody
naranja f	orange
nariz f	nose
nata f	cream

Spanish – English

natación f — swimming
natural — natural; fresh; plain
Navidad f — Christmas
necesario(a) — necessary
necesitar — to need; to require
negarse — to refuse
negocios mpl — business
negro(a) — black
neumático m — tyre
nevar — to snow
nevera f — refrigerator
niebla f — fog
nieto(a) mf — grandson/daughter
nieve f — snow
niña f — girl; baby girl
ningún(a) — none
ninguno(a) —
niño m — boy; baby; child

niños — children (infants)
nivel m — level; standard
Nº — abbrev. for número
noche f — night
esta noche — tonight
Nochebuena f — Christmas Eve
Nochevieja f — New Year's Eve
nombre m — name
norte m — north
Norteamérica f — America; USA
norteamericano(as) — American
nosotros(as) — we
noticias fpl — news
novia f — girlfriend; fiancée; bride
noviembre m — November
novio m — boyfriend; fiancé; bridegroom

nublado(a) — cloudy
nuestro(a) — our; ours
Nueva Zelanda f — New Zealand
nuevo(a) — new
número m — number; size; issue
número de móvil — mobile number
nunca — never

O

o — or
o... o... — either... or...
objetivo m — lens (on camera)
objeto m — object
objetos de valor — valuables
obligatorio(a) — compulsory
obra f — work; play (theatre)
obtener — to get (to obtain)

Spanish – English

océano m	ocean
octubre m	October
ocupado	engaged
oeste m	west
oferta f	special offer
oficina f	office
oficina de Correos	Post Office
ofrecer	to offer
oído m	ear
oir	to hear
ojo m	eye
olor m	smell
operación f	operation
oportunidades fpl	bargains
orden f	command
orden m	order
ordenador m	computer
ordenador portátil	laptop
ordenador de bolsillo	palmtop, PDA
oreja f	ear
organizar	to arrange; to organize
oro m	gold
oscuro(a)	dark; dim
oso m	bear (animal)
otoño m	autumn; fall
otro(a)	other; another
otra vez	again

P

paciente mf	patient (in hospital)
padre m	father
padres	parents
paella f	paella (rice dish)
pagado(a)	paid
pagar	to pay for; to pay
pagar al contado	to pay cash
página f	page
página web	website
Páginas Amarillas fpl	Yellow Pages
pago m	payment
país m	country
paisaje m	landscape; countryside
palabra f	word
palacio m	palace
pálido(a)	pale
palo m	stick; mast
palo de golf	golf club
pan m	bread; loaf of bread
panadería f	bakery
panecillo m	bread roll
pantalones mpl	trousers

Spanish	English
pantalones cortos	shorts
pantys mpl	tights
pañuelo m	handkerchief; scarf
pañuelo de papel	tissue
papel m	paper
papel higiénico	toilet paper
papelería f	stationer's
paquete m	packet; parcel
par	even (number)
par m	pair
para	for; towards
parabrisas m	windscreen
parachoques m	bumper (car)
parada f	stop
parado(a)	unemployed
parador m	state-run hotel
paraguas m	umbrella
parar	to stop
pareja f	couple (2 people)
parque m	park
parque de atracciones	funfair
parquímetro m	parking meter
parrilla f	grill; barbecue
a la parrilla	grilled
particular	private
partido m	match (sport); party (political)
partir	to depart
pasaje m	ticket; fare; alleyway
pasajero(a) mf	passenger
pasaporte m	passport
pasar	to happen
pasatiempo m	hobby; pastime
Pascua f	Easter
¡Felices Pascuas!	Happy Easter!
paseo m	walk; avenue; promenade
pasillo m	corridor; aisle
paso m	step; pace
paso a nivel	level crossing
paso de peatones	pedestrian crossing
paso subterráneo	pedestrian underpass
pasta f	pasty; pasta
pasta de dientes	toothpaste
pastel m	cake; pie
pasteles	pastries
pastelería f	cakes and pastries; cake shop
patata f	potato
patatas fritas	french fries; crisps
peaje m	toll

Spanish - English

Spanish	English
peatón(ona) *mf*	pedestrian
pecho *m*	chest; breast
pechuga *f*	breast (*poultry*)
pedir	to ask for; to order
pedir prestado	to borrow
pegar	to stick (on); to hit
peine *m*	comb
pelar	to peel (*fruit*)
película *f*	film
peligro *m*	danger
peligro de incendio	fire hazard
peligroso(a)	dangerous
pelo *m*	hair
pelota *f*	ball
pelota de golf	golf ball
pelota de tenis	tennis ball
peluquería *f*	hairdresser's
pendientes *mpl*	earrings
pensar	to think
pensión *f*	guesthouse
pensionista *mf*	senior citizen
peor	worse; worst
pequeño(a)	little; small; tiny
pera *f*	pear
perder	to lose; to miss (*train, etc*)
perdido(a)	missing (*lost*)
perdón *m*	pardon; sorry
perdonar	to forgive
perfumería *f*	perfume shop
periódico *m*	newspaper
permitido(a)	permitted; allowed
permitir	to allow; to let
pero	but
perro *m*	dog
persona *f*	person
pesado(a)	heavy; boring
pesar	to weigh
pesca *f*	fishing
pescadería *f*	fishmonger's
pescado *m*	fish
peso *m*	weight; scales
pez *m*	fish
picado(a)	chopped; minced; rough (*sea*); stung (*by insect*)
picadura *f*	insect bite; sting
picante	peppery; hot; spicy
picar	to itch; to sting
pie *m*	foot
piel *f*	fur; skin; leather
pierna *f*	leg
pieza *f*	part; room
pijama *m*	pyjamas
pila *f*	battery (*radio, etc*)
píldora *f*	pill
pimienta *f*	pepper (*spice*)

Spanish	English
pimiento *m*	pepper (vegetable)
piña *f*	pineapple
pinchar	to have a puncture
pinchazo *m*	puncture
pintura *f*	paint; painting
Pirineos *mpl*	Pyrenees
pisar	to step on; to tread on; to keep off the grass
no pisar el césped	keep off the grass
piscina *f*	swimming pool
piso *m*	floor; storey; flat
pista *f*	track; court
plancha *f*	iron (for clothes)
a la plancha	grilled
planchar	to iron
plano *m*	plan; town map
planta *f*	plant; floor; sole (of foot)
planta baja/alta	ground/top floor
plata *f*	silver
plátano *m*	banana; plane tree
plato *m*	plate; dish
plato del día	dish of the day (food); course
playa *f*	beach; seaside
plaza *f*	square (in town)
plaza de toros	bull ring
plazas libres	vacancies
pobre	poor
poco(a)	little
poco hecho(a)	rare (steak)
pocos(as)	(a) few
un poco de	a bit of
poder	to be able
policía *f*	police
Policía Municipal/Local	local police
Policía Nacional	national police
polideportivo *m*	leisure centre
pollo *m*	chicken
polo *m*	ice lolly; polo shirt
pomada *f*	ointment
pomelo *m*	grapefruit
poner	to put
poner en marcha	to start (car)
ponerse en contacto	to contact
por	by; per; through; about
por adelantado	in advance
por correo	by mail
por ejemplo	for example

Spanish – English

Spanish – English

porque	because	presión f	pressure	programa m	programme
portaequipajes m	luggage rack	presión arterial	blood pressure	prohibido(a)	prohibited/no...
portero m	caretaker; doorman	prestar	to lend	prohibido aparcar/ estacionar	no parking
posible	possible	primavera f	spring (season)		
postal f	postcard	primer/o(a)	first	prohibido bañarse	no bathing
postre m	dessert; pudding	primeros auxilios mpl	first aid	prohibido el paso	no entry
potable	drinkable	principal	main	pronto	soon
precio m	price; cost	principiante mf	beginner	pronunciar	to pronounce
precioso(a)	lovely	prioridad (de paso) f	right of way	propiedad f	property
preferir	to prefer			propietario(a) mf	owner
prefijo m	dialling code	privado(a)	private		
pregunta f	question	probador m	changing room	propina f	tip
preguntar	to ask	probar	to try; to taste	propio(a)	own
preocupado(a)	worried	probarse	to try on (clothes)	protector solar m	suncream
preparar	to prepare; to cook	procedente de...	coming from...	próximo(a)	next
presentar	to introduce	productos mpl	produce; products	pueblo m	village; country
preservativo m	condom	productos lácteos	dairy products	puente m	bridge
		profundo(a)	deep		

Left column

puerta f — door; gate
cierren la puerta — close the door
puerta de embarque — boarding gate
puerto m — port
puesto de socorro — first-aid post
puesto que — since
pulpo m — octopus
pulsera f — bracelet
puro m — cigar

Q

que — than; that; which
¿qué? — what?; which?
¿qué tal? — how are you?
quedar — to remain; to be left
quedar bien — to fit (clothes)

Middle column

queja f — complaint
quemado(a) — burnt
quemadura f — burn
quemar — to burn
querer — to want; to love
querer decir — to mean
queso m — cheese
¿quién? — who?
quiosco m — kiosk
quitar — to remove
quizá(s) — perhaps

R

ración f — portion
raciones — portions
radio m — spoke (wheel)
radiografía f — X-ray
rápido m — express train
rápido(a) — quick; fast
raqueta f — racket
rato m — a while

Right column

ratón m — mouse
razón f — reason
real — royal
rebajas tfpl — sale(s)
recambio m — spare; refill
recargar — to recharge (battery, etc)
recibir — to receive
recibo m — receipt
recientemente — recently
reclamación f — claim; complaint
reclamar — to claim
recoger — to collect
recogida de equipajes — baggage reclaim
recomendar — to recommend
recuerdo m — souvenir
reembolsar — to reimburse; to refund
reembolso m — refund

Spanish – English

Spanish – English

refresco *m*	refreshment; cold drink	
regalo *m*	gift; present	
régimen *m*	diet	
región *f*	district; area; region	
registrarse	to register (at hotel)	
regla *f*	period (menstruation); ruler (for measuring)	
Reino Unido *m*	United Kingdom	
reírse	to laugh	
rellenar	to fill in	
reloj *m*	clock; watch	
RENFE *f*	Spanish National Railways	
reparación *f*	repair	

reparar	to repair
repetir	to repeat
reproductor de CD/DVD *m*	CD/DVD player
reproductor MP3 *m*	MP3 player
repuestos *mpl*	spare parts
reserva *f*	booking(s); reservation
reservado(a)	reserved
reservar	to reserve; to book
resfriado *m*	cold (illness)
respirar	to breathe
responder	to answer; to reply
respuesta *f*	answer
resto *m*	the rest
retrasado(a)	delayed
retraso *m*	delay
sin retraso	on schedule

reunión *f*	meeting
revelar	to develop (photos)
revista *f*	magazine
riñón *m*	kidney
río *m*	river
robar	to steal
robo *m*	robbery; theft
rodilla *f*	knee
rojo(a)	red
románico(a)	Romanesque
romper	to break; to tear
ropa *f*	clothes
rosa *f*	rose
rosa	pink
rosado *m*	rosé
roto(a)	broken
rotonda *f*	roundabout (traffic)

rubio(a)	blond; fair haired
rueda f	wheel
rueda de repuesto	spare tyre
rueda pinchada	flat tyre
ruido m	noise
ruta f	route
ruta turística	tourist route

S

sábado m	Saturday
sábana f	sheet (bed)
saber	to know (facts); to know how (to do something)
sacar	to take out (of bag, etc)
sacarina f	saccharin
sal f	salt
sin sal	unsalted

sala f	hall; hospital ward
salado(a)	savoury; salty
salchicha f	sausage
saldos mpl	sales
salida f	exit/departure
salir	to go out; to come out
salmón m	salmon
salsa f	gravy; sauce; dressing
saltar	to jump
salteado(a)	sauté; sautéed
salud f	health
sandalias tfpl	sandals
sandía f	watermelon
sangrar	to bleed
secar	to dry
seco(a)	dry; dried (fruit, beans)

seguida:	
en seguida	straight away
seguido(a)	continuous
seguir	to continue; to follow
según	according to
segundo m	second (time)
segundo(a)	second
seguramente	probably, almost certainly
seguridad f	reliability; security
seguro m	insurance
seguro del coche	car insurance
seguro de vida	life insurance
sello m	stamp (postage)
semáforo m	traffic lights
semana f	week
semanal	weekly

Spanish – English

Spanish - English

Spanish	English
señal f	sign; signal; road sign
sencillo(a)	simple; single (ticket)
señor m	gentleman
Señor (Sr.)	Mr; Sir
señora f	lady
Señora (Sra.)	Mrs; Ms; Madam
señoras	ladies
señorita f	Miss
Señorita (Srta.)...	Miss...
sentarse	to sit
sentir	to feel
separado(a)	separated
septiembre m	September
ser	to be
servicio m	service; service charge
área de servicios	service area
servicio incluido	service included
servicios	toilets
servilleta f	serviette
servir	to serve
seta f	mushroom
sexo m	sex; gender
si	if
sí	yes
sida m	AIDS
sidra f	cider
siempre	always
lo siento	I'm sorry
siga	follow
siga adelante	carry on
siga recto	keep straight on
siguiente	following; next
silla f	chair; seat
silla de ruedas	wheelchair
sillón m	armchair
simpático(a)	nice; kind
sin	without
sin plomo	unleaded
sírvase vd./ ud. mismo	self-service/ help yourself
sitio m	place; space; position; site
sobre	on; upon; about; on top of
sobrio(a)	sober
sociedad f	society, company (business)
Sociedad Anónima	Ltd; plc
socio(a) mf	member; partner (business)
¡socorro!	help!
sol m	sun; sunshine
solamente	only

solicitar	to request	
solo(a)	alone; lonely	
sólo	only	
solomillo m	sirloin steak	
soltero(a) mf	bachelor/spinster	
soltero(a)	single (unmarried)	
sombra f	shade; shadow	
sombrero m	hat	
sombrilla f	sunshade; parasol	
sonido m	sound	
sonreír	to smile	
sonrisa f	smile	
sopa f	soup	
sordo(a)	deaf	
Sr.	abbrev. for señor	
Sra.	abbrev. for señora	

Srta.	abbrev. for señorita
stop m	stop (sign)
su	his/her/its/their/your
suavizante m	hair conditioner; fabric softener
submarinismo m	scuba diving
sucio(a)	dirty
sucursal f	branch (of bank, etc)
suelo m	soil; ground; floor
suelto m	small change
suerte f	luck
¡(buena) suerte!	good luck!
sujetador m	bra
supermercado m	supermarket
sur m	south
surfing m	surfing

surtidor m	petrol pump
sus	his/her/their/your

T

tabaco m	tobacco; cigarettes
tablao (flamenco) m	Flamenco show
TALGO m	Intercity express train
talla f	size
taller m	garage (for repairs)
también	as well; also; too
tampoco	neither
tampones mpl	tampons
taquilla f	ticket office
tarde f	evening; afternoon
tarde	late

Spanish – English

Spanish – English

tarjeta – variado

Spanish – English

Spanish	English
tarjeta f	card
tarjeta de crédito	credit card
tarjeta de débito	debit card
tarjeta de embarque	boarding pass
tasca f	bar; cheap restaurant
taxista mf	taxi driver
taza f	cup
té m	tea
teatro m	theatre
telefonear	to phone
teléfono m	phone
teléfono público	payphone
telesilla m	ski lift; chairlift
televisión f	television
temporada f	season
temporada alta/baja	high/low season
tenedor m	fork (for eating)
tener	to have
tener fiebre	to have a temperature
ternera f	veal
terraza f	terrace; balcony
tiempo m	time; weather
tienda f	store; shop; tent
tienda de ropa	clothes shop
tijeras f/pl	scissors
timbre m	doorbell; official stamp
tintorería f	dry-cleaner's
tío m	uncle
típico(a)	typical
tipo m	sort
tipo de cambio	exchange rate
tirar	to throw (away); to pull
para tirar	disposable
tire	pull
tirita f	(sticking) plaster
toalla f	towel
tobillo m	ankle
tocar	to touch; to play (instrument)
todo(a)	all
todo	everything
todo incluido	all inclusive
tomar	to take; to have (food/drink)
tomar el sol	to sunbathe
tomate m	tomato
tónica f	tonic water
tonto(a)	stupid
torcedura f	sprain
torero m	bullfighter
tormenta f	thunderstorm
toro m	bull
torre f	tower
tos f	cough

Spanish	English	Spanish	English	Spanish	English
toser	to cough	**tubo de escape** m	exhaust pipe	**usar**	to use
tostada f	toast	**tumbona** f	deckchair	**usted**	you (polite singular)
trabajar	to work (person)	**túnel** m	tunnel	**ustedes**	you (polite plural)
trabajo m	work	**turista** mf	tourist	**útil**	useful
traducción f	translation	**U**		**utilizar**	to use
traer	to fetch; to bring	**Ud(s).**	abbrev. for **usted(es)**	**uva** f	grape
traje m	suit; outfit	**últimamente**	lately	**V**	
traje de baño	swimsuit	**último(a)**	last	**vacaciones** f/pl	holiday
tranquilo(a)	calm; quiet	**un(a)**	a/an	**vacío(a)**	empty
transbordo m	transfer	**uña** f	nail (finger, toe)	**vacuna** f	vaccination
tranvía m	tram; short-distance train	**únicamente**	only	**vagón** m	railway carriage
travesía f	crossing	**Unión Europea** f	European Union	**vale**	OK
tren m	train	**universidad** f	university	**válido(a)**	valid (ticket, licence, etc)
trozo m	piece	**unos(as)**	some	**vapor** m	steam
tú	you (singular with friends)	**urgencias** f/pl	A&E, casualty department	**al vapor**	steamed
tu	your (singular with friends)	**urgente**	urgent; express	**vaqueros** mpl	jeans
				variado(a)	assorted; mixed

Spanish – English

Spanish – English

varios(as)	several
vasco(a)	Basque
vaso *m*	glass *(for drinking)*
veces *fpl*	times
vecino(a) *m/f*	neighbour
vehículo *m*	vehicle
velocidad *f*	speed
límite de velocidad	speed limit
velocidad máxima	speed limit
venda *f*	bandage
vendedor(a) *m/f*	salesman/woman
vender	to sell
se vende	for sale
venir	to come
venta *f*	sale; country inn
ventana *f*	window
ventilador *m*	fan *(electric)*
ver	to see; to watch
verano *m*	summer
verdad *f*	truth
¿de verdad?	really?
verde	green
verduras *fpl*	vegetables
vestido *m*	dress
vestirse	to get dressed
veterinario(a) *m/f*	vet
vez *f*	time
viajar	to travel
viaje *m*	journey; trip
viaje de negocios	business trip
viajero *m*	traveller
vida *f*	life
viejo(a)	old
viento *m*	wind
viernes *m*	Friday
viña *f*	vineyard
vinagre *m*	vinegar
vino *m*	wine
violación *f*	rape
violar	to rape
virus *m*	virus
visita *f*	visit
viudo(a) *m/f*	widow/widower
vivir	to live
V.O. (versión original)	undubbed version (of film)
volar	to fly
volver	to come/go back; to return
vosotros	you *(plural with friends)*
vuelo *m*	flight
vuestro(a)	your *(plural with friends)*

W
wáter *m*   lavatory; toilet

Y
y   and
yo   I; me
yogur *m*   yoghurt

Z
zanahoria *f*   carrot
zapatería *f*   shoe shop
zapato *m*   shoe
zumo *m*   juice

Spanish – English

Wifi

Bar Arena

Fiddlers Bar (near church)

Global Bar (Marina)

Vino Blanco (Marina)

The Irish Anvil Bar.